The first decades of the new century have confirmed two features of the predicted trajectory of global Christianity: it continues to grow dramatically in regions that once seemed impervious to the gospel, and its center of gravity is shifting inexorably to the Global South. But these positive developments have also raised challenging questions about how well the church is coping in terms of its responsibility to disciple the estimated 50,000 new believers being added daily.

In this thoroughly researched and well argued work, Dr. Jessy Jaison calls for an urgent critique of the normalization of theological education (TE) as an end in itself, abstracted from the church. Using solid research from the South Asian context, Dr. Jaison asserts that while the formal and the nonformal sectors have been busy debating their relative merits and shortcomings, TE has traditionally marginalized the church. The crucial need is to restore a church-centric TE paradigm, whereby theological educators of all sectors collaborate to strengthen the discipleship, leadership development, and missional effectiveness of the local church, for which Dr. Jaison has proposed the innovative Regional Training Hubs (RTH) model.

I highly commend this invaluable resource for theological educators globally.

Ivor Poobalan, PhD
Principal, Colombo Theological Seminary, Sri Lanka
Co-Chair, Theology Working Group, Lausanne Movement

Here is a book for everyone concerned about the vitality of global theological education, who has noticed its ongoing and recent challenges and shifts, and longs for its renewal, reenvisioning, and reformation. Dr. Jessy is a reflective practitioner with deep experience and appreciation of both formal and nonformal theological education and with an unwavering commitment to theological education in, by, for, and with the church. While her research and perspective are intentionally rooted in and relevant for South Asia, this study deserves global consideration. Her work is an important contribution to contemporary discussions on collaborative relationships between formal and nonformal theological education, on quality assurance, and on the missional character of theological education. It is deeply informed by her qualitative research with respondents from four countries in South Asia. She provides the full text of many responses, providing a fascinating and unique opportunity to hear some thoughtful voices from the South Asian context. Part of the significance of this book is the opportunity to hear firsthand unfiltered, unguarded reflections on theological education and the church from South Asian reflective practitioners. Dr. Jessy affirms the real and potential missional values of the variety and diversity of approaches of theological education – formal, nonformal, informal; all needed to serve the church well, each with its own strengths, contributions, and purposes. But her research suggests that, rather than functioning in parallel, these three sectors need to intentionally collaborate, not in an imposed manner, but in an organic and Spirit-led movement with the church at the center. Dr. Jessy tantalizingly outlines the Regional Training Hubs model, not as a universal solution, but as one way this reenvisioning might be manifested and catalyzed.

Scott Cunningham, PhD
Senior Consultant, Overseas Council

Analysis, critique, and promise characterize Dr. Jessy Jaison's reliable guidance in this volume on the contributions and challenges of two primary sectors in theological education. Through disciplined observation and meaningful conversation, the author calls for collaborative training approaches in, by, for, and with the church – the only entity being built by the Lord Christ himself – to address the deficit of the trained workers in the world's most populous region. I intend to regularly consult this thought leader to enhance pastoral health for the sake of church health, especially where Christ's church is growing.

Ramesh Richard, PhD
President, Ramesh Richard Evangelism and Church Health (RREACH)
Professor, Global Theological Engagement & Pastoral Ministries,
Dallas Theological Seminary, Dallas, Texas, USA

Dr. Jessy Jaison is known as a prolific writer, researcher, and challenger of theological education, its philosophy, practices, and relevance. In this book she addresses vital questions of theological education, its relationship with the church, and the crucial nature of the emerging churches. She has grasped the timely need to train women and men to lead the growing number of new believers among these churches. I highly recommend her work for every theological educator across the spectrum who recognizes and cares to understand that theological education exists for and by, and is of, the church. This book is well researched, comprehensive, and challenging. Dr. Jessy has made the reading lucid and impactful by providing graphs and the interviews that provided the raw material.

I rejoice for her cry that gone are the days of solo endeavors in theological education. Now the Lord is calling the churches and theological institutions to collaborate to equip and meet the dire need of those leading God's people, that the church may be rooted and grounded in the triune God and God's word.

Ashish Chrispal, PhD
Senior Consultant, Overseas Council

Dr. Jessy Jaison's book is a great research project and contribution to theological educators and institutions globally. It extends a biblically grounded and research-based invitation to everyone in the training endeavor to critically revisit the purposes and processes in training. The Regional Training Hubs model she introduces in this incredible and timely contribution instills hope and direction for collaborative theological education to strengthen the church and its mission. I congratulate her on this contribution, and I am sure this book will be used widely and bring great results.

Bal Krishna Sharma, PhD
Principal, Nepal Theological College

Jessy Jaison sounds a clarion call to establish the church at the center of theological education. In the midst of historic shifts in global education, Dr. Jaison engages concepts from educational theory and the grounded perspectives of practitioners to evaluate the potential of various modes of theological education. Her conclusion is sober and sage: wherever the goal of serving the church is left unattended, theological education, irrespective of its pattern, turns into an aimless pursuit. Here is a prophetic voice to heed as church, college, and mission seek to form servants for ministry.

Ernest Clark, PhD
Director of Global Training, United World Mission

Today's church will not remain on mission without more effectively trained leaders. Unless theological education moves meaningfully toward collaborative measures across all sectors, the church tomorrow will be no different than it is today. Jessy Jaison takes the reader on a journey that stimulates the confluence of theological education intending to turn that trajectory. Dr. Jaison's text offers a thoughtful examination of key trends in global theological education relevant to virtually any context as well as South Asia. Considering recent and robust global conversations related to collaboration between all sectors of theological education for the sake of the church, including through ICETE, the reader is challenged in a timely way to think anew about the tensions between sectors that have existed historically. In doing so, Jessy likewise encourages us to become more forward-looking and to embrace opportunities for essential ways to work together. Through her collection of sound data from South Asia, Dr. Jaison's research analysis brings home to the reader through practical considerations how the formal and nonformal sectors not only could, but should, move in greater alignment through their training ministries. If what she presents is applied, even to some degree, churches in South Asia will surely be strengthened and show promise for what intersectional global collaboration might mean for the future for Christ's church. A representative glimpse is offered by Dr. Jaison that will embolden all theological education leaders from all regions to prayerfully reset their collaborative focus and meet the needs of today's church.

Michael A. Ortiz, PhD
International Director, ICETE
Vice President for Global Ministries,
Dallas Theological Seminary, Texas, USA

ICETE Series

Building the Whole Church

Global Hub for Evangelical Theological Education

GLOBAL LIBRARY

Building the Whole Church

Collaborating Theological Education Practices in the Ecclesial Context of South Asia

Jessy Jaison

© 2023 Jessy Jaison

Published 2023 by Langham Global Library
An imprint of Langham Publishing
www.langhampublishing.org

Langham Publishing and its imprints are a ministry of Langham Partnership

Langham Partnership
PO Box 296, Carlisle, Cumbria, CA3 9WZ, UK
www.langham.org

ISBNs:
978-1-83973-859-3 Print
978-1-83973-902-6 ePub
978-1-83973-903-3 PDF

Jessy Jaison has asserted her right under the Copyright, Designs and Patents Act, 1988 to be identified as the Author of this work.

All rights reserved. No part of this publication may be reproduced, stored in a retrieval system or transmitted, in any form or by any means, electronic, mechanical, photocopying, recording or otherwise, without the prior written permission of the publisher or the Copyright Licensing Agency.

Requests to reuse content from Langham Publishing are processed through PLSclear. Please visit www.plsclear.com to complete your request.

Scriptures taken from the Holy Bible, New International Version®, NIV®. Copyright © 1973, 1978, 1984, 2011 by Biblica, Inc.™ Used by permission of Zondervan.

British Library Cataloguing-in-Publication Data
A catalogue record for this book is available from the British Library

ISBN: 978-1-83973-859-3

Cover & Book Design: projectluz.com

Langham Partnership actively supports theological dialogue and an author's right to publish but does not necessarily endorse the views and opinions set forth here or in works referenced within this publication, nor can we guarantee technical and grammatical correctness. Langham Partnership does not accept any responsibility or liability to persons or property as a consequence of the reading, use or interpretation of its published content.

Contents

List of Figures xi

List of Tables xii

Foreword xiii

Acknowledgments xvii

Preface xix

Abstract xxi

1 Introduction: The Shifting Terrain of Theological Education 1

2 A Disadvantageous Gap 21

3 Listening Process 1: Lead Trainers/Faculty in Four Countries in South Asia 51

4 Listening Processes 2–4: Global, Regional, and National Voices 73

5 Thinking Quality, Context, Collaboration, and the Church 99

6 Envisioning Collaboration: A Biblical and Practical Discourse 127

Appendix 1: Defining Formal and Nonformal TE 151

Appendix 2: Opinionnaire 1 155

Appendix 3: Opinionnaire 2 157

Appendix 4: Respondents – Opinionnaires 1 & 2 159

Bibliography 161

List of Figures

Figure 2.2 Making Knowledge and Practice Meet 37

Figure 3.1 Lead Trainers/Faculty Experience in Theological Education 53

Figure 3.2 Student Distribution between NFTE and FTE 54

Figure 3.3 NFTE-FTE Distribution: Lead Trainers and Regional Strategists 54

Figure 3.4 Training Mode Impacting Church Growth 55

Figure 3.5 Leaders Lacking Formal Training 56

Figure 3.6 Concerns around Formal Seminary Education 56

Figure 3.7 Summary Criticisms of FTE 59

Figure 3.8 Concerns around Nonformal Theological Education 59

Figure 3.9 Dimensions of Major Training Needs 62

Figure 3.11 Opinions on Formal-Nonformal TE Collaboration 64

Figure 4.1 South Asia Listening Process Summary 97

Figure 5.1 FTE-NFTE Confluency: Thematic Analysis of the ICETE Dialogue 100

Figure 5.2 NFTE Accreditation Paradigms 108

Figure 5.3 FTE-NFTE Collaborative Symbiotic Paradigm 110

Figure 5.4 Collaborative Vitality of Traditional and Contextual Forms 111

Figure 6.1 Depiction of Church Positioning in TE 138

Figure 6.2 Church-Centered Regional Training Hubs Model 140

Figure 6.3 Regional Training Hubs (RTH): Philosophy and Function 142

Figure 6.4 Church-Centered Hub Operations 144

Figure 6.5 RTH Missional Thrust 145

List of Tables

Table 2.1 Formal, Nonformal, and Informal Training Pathways 30

Table 2.3 Criticisms of Formal and Nonformal Theological Education 38

Table 3.10 Strengths of Formal and Nonformal Modalities 63

Table 3.12 Enhancing Quality in NFTE 70

Foreword

Twenty-five years ago, I visited a house church in western Cuba. During a torrential downpour, I ducked into the back of the house, where I met the pastor and his wife. They brought me into the living room, which had been turned into a sanctuary with a pulpit at the front and wooden benches as pews. A group of thirty to forty young men and women started taking their seats. I assumed that this was the congregation, and that they expected me to preach.

Instead, I started asking questions. I learned that the actual congregation numbered over two hundred and spilled out into the yard outside. These young people had been mobilized by the pastor to plant new house churches in neighboring towns. They were all under thirty years old; they had been Christians for less than five years, had zeal for evangelism, and loved to worship. But they had grown up in officially atheistic schools, had no experience in Sunday school, youth groups, or Christian camps, and no Bible school. But they were leading house churches. Among the challenges they faced was how to preach and teach from the Bible. I asked, "Would it help if I sent a Bible teacher once a month for a week at a time?" They shouted in unison, "*Por favor!*"

I began to see the same dynamic elsewhere as I traveled around the world as a young mission agency leader. The church was exploding with growth, resulting in a burgeoning need for equipping ministry leaders. In many places, they looked to me as the leader of a Western mission organization for solutions – which seemed both puzzling and troubling. When I looked for solid local training materials, I came up empty. In Vietnam, our partner's church planters were being equipped with discipleship materials from a US campus ministry left by a missionary in the 1970s. In northern India, church planters were learning Western systematic theology in preparation for evangelism and discipleship among Hindus! In Senegal, the church planters I saw in a makeshift classroom under a tree looked bored to sleep; something in the pedagogy seemed to be missing.

I wondered: Why are most of the nonformal training materials and programs from the West? Where are the contextual resources? Who is positioned in local contexts to help churches and local missions to develop nonformal training appropriate to the learners? Are the seminaries in these countries part of the solution? Who can help train the trainers for nonformal training? Maybe I was traveling in the wrong circles, but for church planting and mission practitioners at the grassroots level, the cupboard of resources for ministry training seemed to be bare.

In this book, *Building the Whole Church: Collaborating Theological Education Practices in the Ecclesial Context of South Asia*, Dr. Jessy Jaison argues that silos, gaps, and brokenness that hinder effective ministry training persist in South Asia, if not globally. Her work is grounded in this question: "Are there more effective ways to be responsive to the escalating training needs and the challenges faced by the church in our times?" Her answer is a resounding, "*Yes!*"

Dr. Jessy discerns a *kairos* moment in global theological education. She writes with urgency about the convergence of several major shifts that call us to reenvision and renew theological education. The core of the book is a report on her recent qualitative research which engaged leaders and practitioners in four South Asian countries. She listens to these voices alongside the global dialogue on theological education in the Lausanne Movement and International Council for Evangelical Theological Education (ICETE), as well as recent literature on the subject.

Here is an opportunity for the global church to hear the voices of South Asian leaders and practitioners on the current state and preferred future of theological education and ministry training. We learn their perspectives on accreditation, quality assurance, the role of formal and nonformal training, and the place of the church. We also hear possible ways to move from dialogue about needed change to new models and collaborative action. We should listen and pray, wherever we find ourselves in the world.

Jessy is uniquely positioned to research and to speak on the topic of collaboration in theological education. She and her husband, Dr. Jaison Thomas, have thirty years of experience teaching and leading at seminary level in India, with a deep concern as well for nonformal training for the local church and its mission. Jessy has written widely about holistic ministry formation, research, and program design (among other topics). I am blessed to be a coworker with

Jessy through the Overseas Council ministry of United World Mission. She is a strategic thinker, and she leads with conviction, humility, and resolve. Her voice is prophetic.

While focused on the realities of South Asia, this book is important reading for everyone concerned about global ministry training; indeed, for anyone concerned about the vitality of the growing global church and its mission. It envisages a future in which the church is restored to a central role in forming its leaders and in which appropriate collaboration among formal and nonformal theological educators serves the shared goal of equipping the whole church for its mission.

John G. Bernard, DMin
President, United World Mission, USA

Acknowledgments

First and foremost, my gratitude goes to God for his enabling grace, wisdom, and strength that have made this project come to fruition.

This monograph would not have been possible without the support of leaders, colleagues, and research participants around the globe who gladly offered their time to share their challenges and hopes about theological education.

My deepfelt gratitude goes to the United World Mission Overseas Council ministries (UWM-OC) and Dallas Theological Seminary (DTS) for partnering to support this research and writing endeavor. I am forever indebted to Dr. Scott Cunningham for his help at every stage – from finding a conducive study environment to getting the manuscript edited. Being a Scholar-in-Residence at Dallas Theological Seminary gifted me uninterrupted time for learning and reflection. Heartfelt thanks to Dr. Scott and Beth Cunningham for blessing me with your selfless support and the much-needed break amid the months of rigorous research and writing. Thanks to Dr. Michael Ortiz and the Global Ministries at DTS for all the arrangements that made my stay most comfortable during this period of intense work. A special word of thanks also to Dr. Michael and Kathy Ortiz for offering your time amid your busy schedule as I wrestled through ideas and issues in theological education today. Dr. Ramesh Richard has been a great friend and partner in prayer and conversation during this period of writing. A special word of thanks also goes to Dr. Ramesh and Bonnie Richard for their friendship and fellowship.

This project commenced as I was transitioning from my three-decades-long service at the New India Bible Seminary in Kerala, India. I will be forever thankful to the NIBS-NIBC families and to Dr. Alexander and Laly Philip, NIEA, for their sincere association and fellowship in ministry over the past many years.

Several leaders and colleagues have enriched my thinking and sharpened my vision by coming alongside to offer insights, encouragement, and prayer.

A special word of thanks goes to Dr. John Bernard for his insights on Regional Training Hubs and his sincere encouragement in this research project. I am grateful for the support of Dr. Ernest Clark, Rev. Josue Fernandez, Dr. Ashish Chrispal, Mrs. Michelle Lee, and the entire team of UWM and OC. I also want to thank Dr. Ivor Poobalan, Dr. Finny Philip, Dr. William Subash, Dr. Malcolm Webber, Dr. Manfred Kohl, Dr. Graham Aylett, Dr. Theresa Roco Lua, Dr. Bal Krishna Sharma, Dr. Lal Senanayake – and the list goes on.

Thanks to ICETE-Langham Publishing team, and especially Mark Arnold, for the sincere support in getting this work published. After my *Vital Wholeness in Theological Education: Framing Areas for Assessment* published in 2017, I am grateful for another opportunity to partner with Langham Publishing.

My deepest sense of appreciation goes to Dr. Jaison Thomas, my husband, for being my inspiration in life, learning, and service. Thank you for the countless extra miles you walk guiding and supporting me in ministry. Much love to our sons and families, Abraham and Sherin, and Aquil and Krupa, my resolute champions and prayer partners. Thanks to my parents for their constant support in prayer.

Most importantly, my research participants from Sri Lanka, Bangladesh, Nepal, and India are the ones who deserve the loudest shouts of thanks and appreciation. To each of you I am indebted for your time, attentiveness, and genuine participation, without which this study would not have achieved its outcome. While your names are kept anonymous in this work, I continue to pray God's abundant favor on each of you as you toil selflessly in theological education across South Asia. I am grateful that the listening process with you all was incredibly insightful, pointing to the need for collaborative listening and cross-fertilizing leadership patterns. May this lead to the ideation and nourishment of a theological education momentum in the most neglected yet most compelling terrain of the church.

Preface

The original idea was not for a book as such, but for a careful process of listening to theological education practitioners in South Asia regarding the scope for formal-nonformal integration and quality assurance across the streams of training. From my experience in theological education in the region, I have often felt that the training systems are so stuck in their own routines that a revisiting or reenvisioning is often pushed out of the agenda, irrespective of how hard we try. Educational sectors tend to focus more on internal maintenance and academic technicalities than on creative collaborations and outcome-oriented ministry formation in serving the needs of the church. Hence I commenced qualitative research on the context, which eventually led to this book which presents the compelling insights from the study.

Changes are occurring in theological education globally on an unprecedented scale. When gaps between training sectors diminish the impact of training on the mission and growth of the church, we are forced to choose to either "listen and change" or "disregard and die." Participants in this study and the authors cited categorically demand the revitalization of our training practices for the building up of the church. This in no way negates the importance of contextually relevant and well-functioning theological education in seminaries or any other institutional forms. The study suggests that the core mandate of theological education (TE) is to think outside the box of conventionality and serve toward the sustainability and growth of the church. To this end, educators and strategic leaders and administrators in TE are summoned to collaborate or explore new models that effectively address the needs and meet the challenges of the church on the ground.

Presenting a model based on the research, namely the Regional Training Hubs (RTH) in South Asia, this book envisions a "breakthrough collaboration" which will help "the entire land to be irrigated," not just certain sections of it. It advocates for the whole body of the church to be equipped consistently in a vision where the church lives as God's redemptive goal and not as a side actor. Collaboration of all sectors of training is regarded as central to the equipping of the whole church in discipleship, leadership, and mission. The study envisages that such church-focused collaborative models will simultaneously serve to synergize all other forms of theological education. Change or we die. This cannot be overemphasized. Collective wisdom and listening set the way forward. The church as an organic body will keep growing in God's plan, and each generation has to offer strategic spiritual and educational support in context to make it flourish in changing times.

Abstract

There is an enormous dearth of trained leaders in the church, and the exigency to accelerate missional increase across South Asia sets the background to this project. The changing landscape of theological education amid global cultural shifts warrants a conscientious revisiting of the purpose and philosophy of training endeavors. Examining the collaborative prospects of formal and nonformal trainings through a qualitative listening process, this work proposes the church's centrality as a biblical and missional inevitability in theological education. Set in the South Asian context but with a broader relevance, it calls theological educators to make sure that the outcomes of upper-level consultations are trickling down to the church, which is the key agent and the primary stakeholder of training. Having listened to global and local voices, the author examines how the forms of TE have shifted from their goal of church/mission-centeredness, and suggests the Regional Training Hubs (RTH) model as a cogent solution that models polycentric listening and relationship-oriented collaborations. To this end, subsequent action research processes will implement and trial the RTH prototypes in South Asian countries. The future of theological education, irrespective of forms and modalities, must be about envisioning a thriving church by strategically blending spiritual and relational momentums. Institutions and situations keep changing, but the church's mandate stands unaltered. The study recommends genuine listening, persuasive generosity, theological conviction, and relational collaborations toward a church-centered, mission-enhancing theological education paradigm. It envisions all-level discipleship, all-level leadership, and all-level missional-social engagement for the building up of the church, to which, by way of consulting, resourcing, and mentoring, all forms of training endeavors will serve.

1

Introduction: The Shifting Terrain of Theological Education

While formal-nonformal negotiations are fervently taking place, the recent global shifts in theological education (TE) call for a comprehensive definition and reenvisioning of the contexts of the church and mission in South Asia. Theological education that has been taken over by seminaries and then willingly outsourced by churches has grown increasingly disconnected from the church. This is a time-worn lament in literature and consultations, yet the issue remains mostly unresolved on the ground. As the world becomes progressively more globalized, and local settings are beginning to encounter crises of identity and direction, the forward trajectory warrants a more attentive listening to local voices, continued learning, and a complete trust in God. Disengaged strategy-making or enforcement of training packages may have no impact on church growth as the missional scenario is constantly changing. This study supposes that the church on the ground in every community is constrained to own theological or missional wisdom as its vocation. Genuine collaborations of varied forms of theological and ministerial education seem to be crucial for the sustainable thriving of Christianity in the region. The church should be the driver of the theologically grounded mission force to build the kingdom of God among all peoples. And, while a large number of theological institutions keep shifting their training forms and agendas according to sociocultural or political waves, we recognize the church as the only organic agent that can unswervingly fulfill this mandate amid persecution, pandemics, wars, or any other crises that might shake the world.

Major dysfunctions in the formal and nonformal approaches to theological education have historically been identified, and these are explored through the listening process in this study. For theological education to sustain its relevance and effectiveness in a fast-changing world, this study proposes an essential revitalization through a church-focused collaboration of training practices. Across the spectrum of theological education, the study recommends an essential reenvisioning of contextual relevance, quality, and collaboration – all toward the building up of inwardly healthy and missionally vibrant churches.

Let us consider various scenarios.

We need equipped disciples in the church, trained workers in mission, and competent leaders across the leadership spectrum. Traditional seminaries in their scholarly pattern claim to train well, but they can afford to train only a few students. When graduates from conventional seminary education fail to have specific ministry skills in the real world, nonformal initiatives offer help with their flexible patterns of training, yet often without an explicit perception of needs in the real world that are seeking the knowledge base for faith.

The lament over the church-seminary disconnect resounds alarmingly in countries that are relatively new in their Christian tradition and history of theological education, as well as in those with a reasonably lengthy tradition of Christianity, like India. This disconnect develops and solidifies over a period of time and reverberates both ways, as a theological educator remarked:

> Even when churches maintain high regard for formal theological education, they often are unwilling to provide their candidates with a financial or mentoring hand. On the other hand, seminaries have closed their eyes to the missional panorama as their funds are absorbed for the making and maintenance of massive infrastructures and the sustenance of complex educational systems that deny access to the church or the community in the neighborhood.[1]

---

1. Personal interview with a regional TE strategist from South Asia, 26 August 2022. Names of respondents are kept confidential based on the ethical value set in the research.

Where is the gap? We see how the church over many decades has outsourced training to the seminaries, and, on the other hand, the seminaries have assumed discipleship to be an essential task of the church, and both have entrusted the task of soul-winning to the mission organizations. In practice, several links in the chain of discipleship–leadership–mission engagement–church planting–multiplication seem broken: Churches lack a solid discipleship base, seminaries lack pathways to get their graduates back to their churches, and the function of a large number of mission agencies is disconnected from both. Saying this, we affirm discipleship as a lifelong pursuit and not merely as a foundational step that gets one farther on in leadership or mission engagement. Essentially, all these are lifelong processes to be facilitated within a collaborative frame of families, churches, and training initiatives. The gap is perceptible; it creates a gulf that adversely impacts the life and flourishing of the church in South Asia.

> There are no fixed formats or rules now. No classroom, no library, no finances; our seminary system has turned shapeless. Wondering what the future of the world will be like, we may need to open up to any form of training that can get things to work for the students. If the world survives after Covid, we would still need people to preach the gospel, plant churches and lead them at such a difficult time as this.

So said a faculty member in India at the peak of the COVID-19 pandemic. Declining student numbers, upheavals caused by persecution, and digital transitioning were already shaking seminaries prior to the pandemic. When the pandemic hit, the rock-solid academic practices in the traditional seminaries were turned upside down. Disruption and uncertainty challenged the age-old assumptions of indiscriminate acquiescence to conventionality, driving the faculty to adapt to any form of teaching-learning that could get their institutions going.

At the same time, debates on the "theory-practice dichotomy in theological education" have found their way in, additionally seeking to address the rising issue of the leadership deficit in the global church. Some profound issues have emerged: TE becoming very distant from the church; the church's negligence or slackness in discipleship–leadership–mission training, putting its future at risk; the collaboration of multiple forms of TE being unwelcome or unviable in many contexts; the church encountering a risky deficit of competent local leadership; and too many global endeavors making little local impact.

The global and regional scenarios of theological education and the church prompt us to deeper learning and reflection. Traditional seminary settings are known for academic scholarship and credentialing in pertinent knowledge disciplines, while ministry training centers train people to study their Bibles and develop essential skills in ministry. In their simplest definitions, these represent the "formal" and "nonformal" sectors in TE.[2] Critical tensions exist between the two, rarely suggesting complementarity or collaboration in most parts of the region. The way we perceive TE in this discussion will depend on our individual assumptions of its goal, be it scholarship, professional clergy-making, ministry formation, leader development, or a combination of some or all of these. Fundamentally, *ecclesia* is claimed to be the base and focus of all forms of training, and most TE programs are built on the contention that integration of theory and practice is key to effectiveness.

How optimistic and clear-minded are our educators and leaders regarding the shape of theological education in the decades ahead? Are there more effective ways to be responsive to the escalating training needs and challenges of the church in our times?

Theological Education Landscape: Frame of the Research

Neither the *church-seminary gap* nor the *formal-nonformal tension* is new to theological education. The pattern of the church-seminary relationship has been shaped by centuries of Christian interactions, and we have reached a disruptive, disintegrated, and globalized world where truth, transformation, and teaching have become neutral and individualized terms. This research from the South Asian context falls in line with two of the current global discussions: the Global Leadership Challenge (GLC) and the formal-nonformal dialogue.

---

2. *Formal theological education* (FTE) represents the traditional seminary/Bible school education with academic credentialing, while *nonformal theological education* (NFTE) stands for a variety of other forms of training provided by churches/missions for skills development in or for ministry.

The context has, on the one hand, witnessed notable expansions in theological education, and on the other, faced up to multiple challenges:

- Despite significant global and local endeavors, theological education seems to be becoming further distanced from the life and mission of the local church.
- The church's laxity in training disciples, leaders, and missionaries is setting the future of Christianity at risk.
- Legitimate collaboration between FTE and NFTE seems unviable in most contexts and thus we are yet to find a solution to the rising training needs in the church.
- Well-funded programs and initiatives are failing to achieve significant impact in church growth.

Global cultural shifts are impacting theological education and its multiple patterns everywhere. This chapter looks at a few major shifts, namely the Global Leadership Challenge, the impact of globalization, Christianity's center of gravity shifting to the Global South, and the disruptions to TE caused by the COVID-19 pandemic.

From the discussions on the formal-nonformal streams of evangelical TE and their relationship with (or gap from) the church, this research presents voices from the Lausanne Movement, ICETE (International Council for Evangelical Theological Education) triennials, WEA (World Evangelical Alliance) research, and others that have addressed the pertinent need for training in and for the church. It also lays out the distinctions between the formal, nonformal, and informal streams, and interacts with the recent ICETE dialogues.

Listening to the voices in TE is the key thread in this work as opinionnaires, personal interviews, and a focus group were progressively employed to explore the contextual realities: (a) Opinionnaire 1: lead trainers/TE faculty in South Asia (32 from four countries); (b) Opinionnaire 2: regional training strategists (10) in South Asia; (c) focus group (6 experienced national trainers/educators in South Asia); and (d) personal interviews with global TE leaders (8).

The work navigates through the FTE-NFTE collaboration dialogues, seeking to identify what the leadership and training needs of the church are, and how to find amicable solutions in a fast-changing world of education and

Christian engagement. Helpful and contextually relevant measures are thought through for the areas of South Asia where the gospel is spreading rapidly. How can we keep the church steadily deepening and thriving in its life and mission this century? How far do the current training patterns and practices help in realizing this goal in the region?

The Crossroads: Shifts Warranting a Reenvisioning

The leadership-deficit statistics and the TE dichotomy dialogues should be viewed in the context of a global scenario characterized by extensive sociocultural transitions, some of which are as follows (in no particular order):

1. Global Leadership Challenge (GLC)
2. Globalization
3. Shift in the center of gravity of Christianity to the Global South
4. Disruption and demands caused by the COVID-19 pandemic

Both the church and the seminary are situated in tangible cultural grounds; they do not function in sociocultural neutrality. Whether the cultural waves impact for good or bad, these institutions are obliged to permeate society by confident and responsible witnessing. As Wright says, theologians and theological educators are those who find ways to mend the "broken signposts of the ancient faith"[3] in a rapidly changing world which is heading to a future that is totally different from the past. It is this end that all forms of training are supposed to serve. The global shifts and trends continue to impact – subtly or obviously – the way we perceive and practice theological education today.

The Global Leadership Challenge (GLC)

The recent awakening over the Global Leadership Challenge (GLC) has fueled the discussions over FTE-NFTE today. Gordon-Conwell's Center for the Study of Global Christianity (CSGC) estimates that only 5 percent of the total of 5 million pastors or priests are likely to have had formal theological training.

---

3. N. T. Wright, *Broken Signposts: How Christianity Makes Sense of the World* (New York: HarperOne, 2020). Exploring John's gospel, Wright articulates how the seven broken signposts – justice, love, spirituality, beauty, freedom, truth, and power – could be restored as genuine signposts of Christianity in today's world.

"Roughly 70 percent of these pastors are in Independent congregations. Independent pastors, in particular, have little theological training, even in the West."[4] Zurlo's *Global Christianity* affirms these statistics with supportive evidence.[5] We observe the following:

Since GLC figures are alarming, they warrant a practical response on leadership formation by every Christian entity

Quantitative analysis demonstrates that 2.2 million Protestant pastors in the Majority World lack formal biblical training; 90 percent of churches worldwide are led by brothers and sisters in Christ who have had no formal training; and 50,000 people accept Christ every day in the Majority World, creating a need for a thousand pastors daily.[6] Although many debate the generalizability of the statistics, the need for better-equipped disciples and more trained leaders stands out as an irrefutable reality. That 90 percent of churches in the world are led by men and women with little or no training for ministry[7] is perplexing to those who value the impact of good theological training on individuals and their ministries.

The GLC figures must first drive us to the need for discipleship in the church

Many of the resources in leadership training are wasting away as we try to form leaders without ensuring their lifelong discipleship in the church. These problems are not new; they have always been part of the journey. McGavran observed in 1969, "The insistence on traditional theological education runs the grave danger of dooming a denomination to petty discipling . . . Theological education around the world must fit the economic and educational standards

---

4. Gordon-Conwell Seminary, "Frequently Asked Questions," accessed 6 July 2022, https://www.gordonconwell.edu/center-for-global-christianity/research/quick-facts/.
5. Gina A. Zurlo, *Global Christianity: A Guide to the World's Largest Religion from Afghanistan to Zimbabwe* (Grand Rapids: Zondervan, 2022).
6. Ashish Chrispal, "Theological Education: Which Way?," in *Be Focused . . . Use Common Sense . . . Overcome Excuses and Stupidity*, eds. Reuben van Rensburg, Zoltan Erdey, and Thomas Schirrmacher (Bonn: Verlag für Kultur und Wissenschaft, 2022), 180.
7. United World Mission, "Our Mission," accessed 6 July 2022, https://uwm.org/about/our-mission/.

of the population being evangelized."[8] Schirrmacher speaks of biblical illiteracy among evangelical Christians today, articulating the leadership crisis in the rural pockets of Christianity:

> So many people are becoming believers that the one who has been a believer the longest becomes the leader of the church . . . That might be three years. Short for us, but long for them. We have such a high conversion rate worldwide, that it's extremely difficult to follow up with discipling, with teaching, with Bible knowledge. The result is that people know much less and are . . . much more open to secularism and strange things like the "health and wealth" gospel.[9]

These realities point to the crisis not just in leader-level equipping, but in the discipleship-level building of the church. In spite of the number of seminaries and training initiatives, several areas in the southern hemisphere are faced with the challenges in discipleship and leadership formation. More and more Christlike, Word-grounded leaders are needed where the church continues to grow at the speed of a bullet train, yet the discipleship and leadership training moves like a bullock cart. Why does this situation prevail despite the multiplicity of formal and nonformal trainings? Is it that theological education fails to build leaders for the churches in places where the leaders are most needed? Or is it that the discipleship base of the church is not preparing committed leaders to serve in mission?

We see churches trusting seminaries for the formation of their leaders, and seminaries tend to claim that they are equipping leaders for the multifaceted ministries of the church. Critical gaps were identified long ago and resolutions have long been recommended, yet they have yielded no significant practical results. We recognize that no single institution can effectively tackle this massive

---

8. Donald A. McGavran, "Foreword," in *Theological Education by Extension*, ed. Ralph D. Winter (Pasadena: William Carey Library, 1969), xiii–xiv.

9. Bishop Thomas Schirrmacher is the Secretary General of the World Evangelical Alliance, leading 600 million evangelicals around the globe. Milton Quintanilla, "World Evangelical Alliance Leader Warns That 'Bible Knowledge Is Fading Away,'" Christian Headlines, 4 December 2020, https://www.christianheadlines.com/contributors/milton-quintanilla/our-biggest-problem-is-that-bible-knowledge-is-fading-away-world-evangelical-alliance-leader-warns.html.

leadership deficit; legitimate dialogues have to occur in strategic partnerships, guided by prayer and absolute trust in the divine mandate.

The matter of concern is both the methods and the grounds of leadership training. At least for some, the church's leadership crisis is most effectively resolved by building up its discipleship base in the first instance. For them, leadership created in a vacuum or endowed outside the context of the church, which is the faith community, could be perilous. Sustainable leadership formation is not only divinely favored, but also is contextually endorsed and flourishes organically. Although seminary education is generally an essential requirement for top leadership roles in the church, theological credentials devoid of solid discipleship formation could be counterproductive when it comes to leadership. The gap is formed when the seminary builds its training on the assumption that its students have gained solid discipleship foundations in faith and life. Leader multiplication has to happen concurrently with disciple multiplication and mission multiplication, lest we end up with many leaders with only a handful of believers, or many professors with just a few students! The GLC calls every training institution and the church to critical self-evaluation. The church cannot survive without trained leaders; therefore, we need to listen more on how to resolve the GLC issue in local contexts. We must think: What should the leadership vision for TE in South Asia be if it is to focus on the church's spreading of the Word and on people being added daily from "outside the walls of Christianity"?

Globalization Impacting Theological Education

Globalization is a term used to describe how the processes of trade, technology, education, and so on, have made the world into a more open, interdependent, and connected place. It causes local contexts to become increasingly exposed to and integrated with international or global contexts. Like other sectors, theological education has gained a global reach with strategic goals and networks and is no longer restricted to local siloed practices. The following are a few observations of the impact of globalization on local TE settings in South Asia.

Globalization, though subtly, tends to remove certain fundamental elements of contextual TE

The concern in TE is over how globalization impacts and shapes the content and direction in contexts where the church should flourish. In a global village that sells content and even resource personnel for free for known or unknown partnership advantages, TE faculty often lack guidance as to what to choose and what not, although, of course, some may not mind about this. The foundations of faith also go unattended and ignored, as content becomes generic and sweeping. Values of the local faith culture and vernacular efficiency in mission are overlooked in a culturally transcendent, exclusively English-medium globalized learning culture. According to Douglas, for there to be a renewal, TE must focus beyond its operational issues and start reexamining its commitments in the light of fundamental beliefs and values. For her, the four fundamental roots of globalized TE are *missio Dei*, spiritual formation, the missional nature of the church, and hermeneutical communities.[10] A plethora of consultations and commissions on "the true foundation and purpose of TE" fills the historical records, yet most local contexts seem to be ill-equipped or unwilling to put things into practice on their own initiative. Success "up there" becomes a failure when it loses its connection to the ground. This gap is paralyzing the local church. An authentic revisiting of contextual TE practices will help us see how the expansion, democratization, and deepening of these will benefit us locally.

Globalization infuses a tech-oriented TE where biblical theology and mission get pushed to the margins

To compete with the globalized context, many seminaries seem to be changing their administrative setting in a tech-oriented direction. But when forms and functions change, goals also might change. One of the dilemmas is: Is it a globalized content or methodology, or both, that a local context of TE is being required to embrace? We know that TE is not just a methodology; it has a solid core that should shape the life and mission of the church. Yet there

---

10. Lois McKinney Douglas, "Globalizing Theology and Theological Education," in *Globalized Theology: Belief and Practice in an Era of World Christianity*, eds. Craig Ott and Harold A. Netland (2nd printing; Grand Rapids: Baker Academic, 2007), 274–85.

is a growing fear of a theology-free theological education and a churchless Christianity. When things shrink down to technical skills, technology, statistics, and reports, our academic systems (and mission) get further distanced from the church and its meaningful permeation of the world. Theological education initiatives in local settings may need to review what they are gaining and losing by being tossed by the waves of globalization. Digital technology is taking over, contextual sensitivities are less appreciated, diversified models are emerging, microcosmic learning is giving way to globalized strategies – and amid the confusion we continue to craft plans based on agendas that do not really matter to an ordinary believer in the church who wants to learn the Bible and serve in mission.

The "bad global" widens disparities between the Global North and South

Alongside its powerful effects in the economic, sociopolitical, and religious realms, globalization has altered education and its fundamental assumptions of linear, monotrack, monocultural, institutional, and scholarly pursuits. It has challenged the long-sustained assumptions of formal educational systems and caused the fading or dissolving of their boundaries. However, "globalization" is a disputed concept in its two distinct connotations: what Vanhoozer calls "good global" and "bad global." In the "good global" sense, globalization provides "a planetary consciousness, a deepened awareness of, and sensitivity to, the reality of increasing interdependence among the peoples of the world."[11] The "bad global," on the other hand, is a "homogenizing process, the counterpart in culture and the marketplace to the notion that the Western university is a place of *generic* human learning."[12] In the field of theological education there are disparities between the Global North and South, and there always will be. Non-Western theologies tend to be sidelined as irrelevant to mainstream theologizing, perhaps due to the lack of academic sophistication expected elsewhere, as Ott explains. For him, "profundity is not to be equated with scholarly erudition . . . Such resistance in the Western academy must be overcome if mutual respect,

---

11. David K. Clark, *To Know and Love God: Method for Theology* (Wheaton: Crossway, 2003), 101.
12. Kevin J. Vanhoozer, "One Rule to Rule Them All? Theological Method in an Era of World Christianity," in Ott and Netland, *Globalized Theology*, 99. Emphasis original.

dialogue, and a genuine globalization of theology are to be advanced."[13] Hence globalization of TE may need to continue with an emphasis on "decolonizing" and realizing a balanced intersection of "glocalization," a way in which people in a local context respond to the global. One of the factors that distances FTE from local churches or contextual NFTE initiatives is its indiscriminate embracing of the "bad global" in its academic pursuits.

Globalization puts contextual TE at risk by promoting an ethical and spiritual vacuum

Indiscriminate use of learning materials available "out there" is said to promote an ethical vacuum, doctrinal neutrality, and cultural identity confusion, and the logical approach of the Enlightenment era is nurturing more individualism and little interdependence. But at the core of our thinking is the value of interdependence, an essential component in making the mission of TE whole. Genuine collaboration in theological education or mission does not mean one partner prescribing to another the "what" and "how" of arriving at the goal. Identifying this prevalent tension, Pobee wrote, "Intellectual pursuit may not be the only criterion of excellence in theology in a context of globalization."[14] The hybridity and commodification of education are boosted by globalization. Local ceases to be local. When global paints the local, the level of contextual integration of TE that can be imagined becomes a challenge. What are the effects of this on TE's service to the church in the local setting? Are there areas of caution for schools in the sharing of approaches, resources, and momentum in hybrid and virtual forms? Samuel warns about possible ethical blankness and the resultant violence that could be triggered by the currency of power, and yet he optimistically affirms,

> Our task as theological educators is to avoid a homogenous one size fits all approach, which is one of the drives of globalization, and instead, both embrace our connectedness and use our

---

13. Craig Ott, "Globalizing Theology," in *Globalized Theology*, 334.
14. John S. Pobee, "Theology in the Context of Globalization," 18–26 in *Ministerial Formation* 79 (Oct. 1997): 20.

resources jointly in such a way as to enhance the significance of Christian public witness in each locality.[15]

High-level globalized TE partnerships do not reach down to impact the masses of the less privileged and poor in the Majority World, who often make up the actual mission force of the local church

It is a great thing that global partnerships are increasingly opening up international educational opportunities for anyone, anywhere. Nonetheless, such are said to be mostly inaccessible to those at the societal margins and they are making the church lose most of its key thinkers and teachers who do not return to their original localities after receiving education overseas. This has been a persistent problem in South Asia, with its implied neglect of less privileged believers who need to be equipped for service. While educational opportunities in the West are desirable and valuable, the "brain drain" that results further weakens local mission. Large numbers of scholars and faculty do not return to serve their home countries and villages after their period of education in the affluent West. The Western input in selfless missionary endeavors in the past, and its contributions to women's education, English education, community development, vocational training, and funding assistance have undoubtedly been significant in the growth of Christianity around the world. Seminaries in many Western nations that are themselves struggling to survive are opening up more partnerships and enrolling a great bulk of students from the rest of the world in their programs. We also see new initiatives emerging where nonformal learners are integrated in large numbers into the traditional academic systems. However, FTE in the region of South Asia tends to benefit those who can afford the high costs, are proficient in English, and belong to the urban or semi-urban classes in society. Now, most online NFTE also seems to be following this trend, whereby the poor, tech-illiterate, and the local continue to remain on the fringes.

---

15. Vinay Samuel, "Globalization and Theological Education," in *Christianity and Education: Shaping Christian Thinking in Context*, eds. David Emmanuel Singh and Bernard C. Farr (Eugene: Wipf & Stock, 2011), 89.

When TE settings are impacted by globalization on multiple fronts, the church becomes more isolated and disintegrated in terms of its direction and mission. We must continue to probe as to how to build strong training foundations in South Asia to hasten the missional momentum in churches and marketplaces.

The Shift in the Center of Gravity to the Global South

A big leap in the Christian movement occurred in the last two decades of the twentieth century, with the result that the large majority of Christians are now to be found in what used to be called the "Third World." As Zurlo records:

> Christianity is the world's largest religion; with over 2.5 billion members, it comprises 32% of the global population . . . One of the major features of World Christianity is its shift from the global North (Europe and North America) to the global South (Asia, Africa, Latin America, Oceania) . . . By the year 2050, an estimated 77% of Christians will live in the global South (39% in Africa).[16]

Trainers across the spectrum of ministry are encouraged or even constrained to embrace alterations and adaptations in their modes of training in view of this shift. Nonetheless, we cannot simply overlook the fact that the massive expansions and movements have integral nonformal or informal elements. At the same speed they can spread solid or flawed teachings.

With the shift in Christianity's center of gravity come the strengths and flaws of proliferating informal, independent Christian communities or teachings

Accompanying the global center-of-gravity shift there has also been a power shift that has changed the focus from hierarchies and institutions to the ordinary, grassroots church people who in fact champion the shift. A primary example is Latin America's Pentecostal churches, "whose dynamic life and

---

16. Zurlo, *Global Christianity*, 3. Compare Philip Jenkins's assertion that by 2050, the center of gravity of the Christian world will have shifted firmly to the southern hemisphere, in *The Next Christendom: The Coming of Global Christianity* (Oxford: Oxford University Press, 2007).

witness have been generated almost without formal theological education."[17] Zurlo says that a major feature of Christianity's shift to the Global South "is the rise of Pentecostal/Charismatic Christianity, which at less than 1% in 1900 was at 26% in 2020 and is estimated to be at 30% by 2050."[18] The nontraditional, nonformal approaches in mission and church planting have accelerated the spread of Pentecostal/charismatic Christianity. No conventional seminary system could have afforded to train the number of workers these movements have mobilized to meet the needs of evangelization. For decades we have been observing the immense challenges faced by the fields of religion and theological studies in the Global North. While on the one hand a fading Christian identity in the Euro-American West creates a kind of anxiety in training enterprises elsewhere regarding the sustainability of traditional churches, on the other hand the unguarded spread of independent Christian groups forms a different set of concerns, in spite of the vast majority of them being the frontline evangelistic force of Christianity. In many European countries religious affinities in terms of belief, attendance, and vocation are fading away, what Jenkins originally termed the "wholesale dechristianization," although later he carefully distinguished between institutional Christian practice and the survival of Christian belief among small groups of believers.[19] This shift points to the rising nonformalism in the growth of Christianity. It seems vital to integrate an understanding of the formal and nonformal nature of the church to inform our dialogues on formal and nonformal TE. Because of Christianity's center-of-gravity shift and the West's growing indifference to Christianity, some identify the godless worldviews embedded in postmodernism, and others the exponential impact of the charismatic and Pentecostal movements that have changed the course of history in Majority World Christianity, with their nonformal, mission-oriented, and socially engaging approaches. While the incredible spread owes much to the informal faith communities and their training, there seem to be many rising concerns, particularly with regard to solidity and sustainability.

---

17. F. Ross Kinsler, "Theological Education by Extension: Equipping God's People for Ministry," in *Ministry by the People: Theological Education by Extension*, ed. F. Ross Kinsler (Maryknoll: Orbis, 1983), 2–3.
18. Zurlo, *Global Christianity*, 3.
19. Jenkins, *Next Christendom*, xiii.

The missional focus is perceptibly declining in global TE and this raises concerns over the stability and growth momentum of Christianity in South Asia

Ott explains Bosch's observation of the center of gravity of missiological interest moving from ecumenically oriented universities to evangelically oriented schools.[20] Since the late nineteenth century, mission studies have been under dual tension: While there has been an increasing awareness of the significance of missiological studies, there has been a reluctance of TE schools to provide them with an identity in their curricula.

> The gradual disappearance of missions or missiology from the curriculum of one theological institution after another further emphasizes the malaise. In some of the older European and American faculties of theology, where in the early part of this century missiology appeared to be firmly entrenched, the chairs have been abolished or converted into others for World Christianity, Ecumenical Studies, Third World Theologies, World Religions and the like.[21]

Similar reflexes are already perceptible in South Asian TE, and unless this is addressed with necessary missional urgency, the missional momentum and resultant church growth might be at risk. With the indiscriminate adaptation of educational and missional methods from elsewhere, local cultures often find themselves in confusion. Churches and theological institutions in South Asian nations are minority-labeled entities neglected and oppressed by fanatics of the majority religions. There is a glaringly obvious decline in institutional church practices; the missional agenda of the church is being overridden by the waves of postmodern worldviews and, more recently, by the repercussions of the COVID-19 pandemic.

Ministry training and theological education historically have assumed key roles in the missional momentum of any region. However, what actually

---

20. Bernhard Ott, "Mission Oriented Theological Education: Moving beyond Traditional Models of Theological Education," in Singh and Farr, *Christianity and Education*, 54.
21. David Bosch, "Theological Education in Missionary Perspective," *Missiology* 10, no. 1 (1982): 13–14.

triggered the shift in the center of gravity, how ministry training and theological education work among the local communities, and what the actual role of TE, if any, could be, have always been complex issues. Being obliged to guard and hasten the spread of the gospel in the vast region of South Asia, we must delve deeper into the culture, local needs, the church's stature, and biblical grounding, and thus craft the way forward. This warrants a shift in mindset from the set curriculum to a responsive rendering. There is a growing awareness of the necessity to get beyond the formal-nonformal tension to focus on the need of the church to continue growing and multiplying. The word of God must spread, and new believers must be added daily as in the Acts narrative; it must keep permeating societies, marketplaces, and religions with conviction and vibrancy.

The Pandemic: Shaken Ivory Towers

The COVID-19 pandemic altered the course of education and, theological education in an unprecedented way. Seminaries explored new ways to survive and adapted by making changes in their modes of design and delivery. Distinct contextual needs and challenges surfaced as residential programs were halted, calling for drastic shifts in attitudes, skills, and practices in doing theological education.

The pandemic season endorsed the significance and feasibility of diversified modes of learning

Though reluctantly, formal seminary systems tested all types of learning, such as distance, remote, blended, online, and cohort studies. Admission pre-requisites were lessened; fees were lowered – at least for a while "until things get back to normal." Ivory towers started shaking when classroom learning stopped and diversified methods had to be adapted. The push to stand barefoot on the rough ground was unexpected, and it came on an unprecedented scale. For a short time eyes were opened to see human realities, especially learners' lived realities in the Majority World, and real-time dialogues locally and globally were initiated to address the enormous ministry needs all around. In other words, the multicolored fabric of Christian training had to interweave complementarity and solidarity for responsiveness and survival. The crisis called the world of the thinkers to see things with an open eye, to listen with a receptive ear, and to feel with a sensitive heart. In retrospect, people have compared the spending on massive infrastructures and its actual impact on the mission of the church in their societies. At the same time, many, feeling suffocated, wished desperately to get back to the comforts of the classroom and to the elevations of the "thinking world."

The digital transition has stimulated a research and learning dimension with key events and writings. The 2022 Triennial Assembly of Asia Theological Assembly (ATA) worked around the theme with theological educators on making sense of the digital experience in learning, and affirmed that "learning needs in a digital age demand more interactivity, context sensitivity, and deep relationality – tasks that call for greater collaboration and collective responsibility within the theological education community."[22] All churches and religious communities are deliberating over the use and misuse of technology in education, as well as in all other dimensions of life. Campbell remarked that religious communities have agency and are actively negotiating how to use, adapt, or reject technology.[23]

The pandemic-stricken world reminded us that theological questions ultimately come to the local church, which is the place of true belonging for the Christian believer

The pandemic brought a sense of awakening that theology and theologizing are properties of churches, missionaries, and mission agencies as much as of the seminaries and theologians. Through the pandemic, the methods and manner of theological education changed, fundamental assumptions regarding *ecclesia* and seminary were challenged, and the deteriorating passion for faith and learning became more evident. Methodological variety in education and training became a high priority for the church's growth and expansion in a shuddering world. The pandemic raised challenging questions regarding faith, life, and God, and shook the systems of church and seminary to their core. Traditions, celebrations, and rituals that held the faith community together disappeared. The younger generation who searched for peace, meaning, and

---

22. Rei Lemuel Crizaldo, "Asian Theologians Consider the Digital Turn in Theological Education," report from the 2022 Triennial Assembly of the Asia Theological Association (ATA), Penang, September 2022, in *WEA Theological News* 51, no. 4 (Oct. 2022): 2.
23. Heidi Campbell, *When Religion Meets New Media* (Abingdon: Routledge, 2010).

identity in digital resources still seem reluctant to return to church services. There may never before have been a moment in many of our lifetimes like this, when every assumption of faith and every foundation of mission was challenged to this extent, similar to a war scenario. Textual theology had to imagine new ways to communicate to people in extreme suffering.

The pandemic set the challenge to adapt to the digital transformation and explore how this might facilitate the church's social and evangelistic engagement with the society

The pandemic dramatically altered the course of ministry and learning engagements. ATA deliberated on certain action points for theological education, namely

> (a) the need to affirm the real and lasting human connections possible in digital spaces, (b) the importance of ensuring that educational design and outcomes drive the learning process more than the technological innovations do, (c) the need to stress authenticity and integrity to keep us human and humane in the digital environment, (d) and a warning not to romanticize the pre-digital life or being too highly digital, since every iteration of technology from the printing press to the metaverse offers both opportunity and pitfalls for the cause of the Gospel.[24]

Regarding the radical cultural changes we are witnessing in the wake of the digital transformation, a Lausanne Occasional Paper suggests,

> rather than seeing digital technology as competition it can be used to supplement and augment existing church [and learning] practices . . . There are . . . larger contextual questions of how faith is shaped and communicated in societies saturated by technology. How to remain a faithful witness in a digital age is something that

---

24. Crizaldo, "Digital Turn in Education," 2.

the church will have to continue to grapple with in the years to come.[25]

Disparities in digital literacy and discussions on theological concerns over the digital transformation within churches and TE project multiple prospects and problems which require significant attention in the journey forward.

While TE faculty had to cope with the sudden loss of traditionally assigned control over the learners, students in TE found themselves

- learning online vs. learning in a library
- learning in isolation vs. learning in community
- learning for real needs vs. learning theories
- learning in doing ministry vs. learning in preparation for ministry

Teachers, pastors, leaders, and missionaries alike felt lost in their homiletic capacity while preaching to an audience not physically present before them; they felt vulnerable at the mounting need to reach out to the dying and the bereaved even as their own lives were under threat from the virus; they needed content and method while facing children, adolescents, and adults who started questioning God, faith, and the Bible. The pandemic crisis extended a disguised invitation to the entire enterprise of TE to assume its rightful vocation in equipping the whole people of God to live and serve. It taught how and why learning should not be separated from life. The gap between learning and life's realities thus calls for advanced deliberations. As Edwin Friedman puts it:

> Conceptually stuck systems cannot become unstuck simply by trying harder. For a fundamental reorientation to occur, that spirit of adventure which optimizes serendipity, and which enables new perceptions beyond the control of our thinking processes, must happen first.[26]

---

25. Jonas Kurlberg, Nam Vo, and Sara Afshari, "Being Church in a Digital Age," Lausanne Occasional Paper for the Theology Working Group, accessed 31 October 2022, https://lausanne.org/content/lop/lausanne-occasional-paper-being-church-in-a-digital-age?fbclid=IwAR2pwpH9lD1HE_3YSYJ_n7HGlyVRIiv9TbpfruzMbgXyOmJ0kE1ARKu70DM.

26. Edwin H Friedman, *A Failure of Nerve: Leadership in the Age of the Quick Fix* (New York: Church Publishing Inc., 2017).

2

A Disadvantageous Gap

As discussed, alongside the gaps between FTE and NFTE is TE's diminishing impact on the mission advancement of the church. Admitting that there are dimensions where training becomes irrelevant and irresponsive, in this chapter we attempt to expound the issues in depth.

Where does the seminary stumble? Timothy Dearborn, of World Vision International, writes:

> I am coming to the conclusion that there is no other professional organization in the world which allows its primary professional institutions to produce graduates who are generally as functionally incompetent as the church permits her seminaries. Most pastors feel unprepared by their seminary education for the demands of pastoral ministry. Can you imagine a medical school retaining its certification if its graduates' first exposure to surgery was as the surgeons? . . . Tragically, that's the scenario most of our seminaries and theological schools are still following . . . Eager students entrust three years of their lives to a seminary in order to be better equipped to love God, people and the world, yet too often they graduate feeling spiritually cold, theologically confused, biblically uncertain, relationally calloused and professionally unprepared.[1]

Where does nonformal training stumble? The president of a seminary in the South Asia region commented,

---

1. Timothy Dearborn, "Transforming Theological Education through Multi-Institutional Partnerships," in *Christianity and Education: Shaping Christian Thinking in Context*, eds. David Emmanuel Singh and Bernard C. Farr (Eugene: Wipf & Stock, 2011), 33.

> Nonformal trainings tend to be occasional events, in many cases. They don't often build up on clear foundations or lead toward a holistic goal. It has learning but cannot be equaled with formal education which has a basis, progression, and direction. Nonformal theological education provides little knowledge and that sets the biggest risk to the church in many countries, with the proliferation of cults and heresies.[2]

Several thousand students graduate annually from FTE yet the churches and missions are still facing an immense shortage of trained leadership. The blame game continues between seminary education and field-based education. Yu articulates the common complaints about seminaries that often fail to turn out effective pastors for ministry and whose curricula are out of touch with the vitality of church life in worship, in spiritual nurture, in helping Christians to practice discipleship in the workplace, and in enhancing mission commitment:

> Seminaries are expected to train leaders; instead, they produce for the church certified professionals armed with fragmented theological ideas and lifeless Biblical interpretative tools honed for critical discourses among scholars who have no interest in the Bible as the Word of God. Seminaries are expected to be the "nursery" or "seed-bed" (*seminarium*) for nurturing spiritual leadership, but they have become "broken cisterns and exhausted wells," for their heavy academic curricula and critical approach manage only to dissipate the spiritual vitality and enthusiasm that young seminarians originally have.[3]

Verifying and addressing this disconnect in context is vital for the renewal of TE.

---

2. Personal interview, Interviewee LTF# 25, 13 August 2022.

3. Carver Yu, "Engaging the Ecclesial Dimension: Theological Education That Empowers the Church," in *The Pastor and Theological Education: Essays in Memory of Rev. Derek Tan*, eds. Siga Arles, Lily Lim, Tan-Chow Mayling, and Brian Wintle (Singapore: Trinity Christian Center & ATA Bangalore, 2007), 167.

Pathways in Theological Education

Winter commented on the position and purpose of nonformal initiatives in TE:

> The traditional seminary had become two things: a) a community of scholars carrying on research as professional academicians, and b) a place where candidates for the ordained ministry (and Christian scholarship) are trained. The extension seminary does in no way intend to replace or play down the first crucial function but it does intend to operate parallel to the latter by a new method which allows a wider, perhaps superior selection of students (as well as large number), training them for ministry whether scholarly or pastoral or both.[4]

Law observed that there are crucial issues that nonformal education needs to address:

> The danger of non-formal TE is that many of them do not have standards to go by or any means of evaluation. Some of the non-formal programs lack a biblical and historical-theological anchor. There is the danger of being driven by immediate issues, moving with a lack of perspective and the lack of a community that can "speak the truth in love."[5]

As a TE consultant in South Asia remarked,

> Informal is not a separate sector in education, it should not be. Both formal and nonformal education are impacted for good or bad by what the learner experiences informally in or outside of the program. By creating sectors we keep making more gaps. Informal learning underpins all-life learning and it cannot be distinguished as an educational continuum.[6]

---

4. Ralph D. Winter, *Theological Education by Extension* (Pasadena: William Carey Library, 1969),xvii.
5. Samuel Law, "Safeguarding the Church," Forum Comment, 17 November 2022, ICETE Academy Forum, ICETE Online Event, November 2021.
6. Interview with a TE consultant in South Asia, 19 September 2022.

Perceptions of these forms vary from person to person. In the following section we discuss these three streams in TE to help further discourse on collaboration.

The Formal, Nonformal, and Informal

By the classification of formal, nonformal, and informal, we are not dividing up knowledge, rather only specifying the context in which knowledge is produced and shared. Learning cannot be divided and it should not be; when compartmentalized it produces only a partial effect. We have been noting how global TE is becoming more convinced of the intrinsic problems it has inherited from the siloed style of theological education, which resulted as a by-product of Aristotelian reasoning logic and the modern university model of the eighteenth-century Enlightenment era. Despite well-intended dialogues and the conviction that a blend of the formal, nonformal, and informal is essential for a transformative impact on the whole person, our bureaucracies have shaped us to think in terms of categories and compartments, and to habitually elevate one form over another. By recognizing and appreciating the distinctiveness of each form of education within the frame of their integrative impact, we guard against unhelpful stereotyping. Jusu comments, "Each approach to theological education has its own niche and its own contribution."[7] The following paragraphs attempt to clarify the distinct approaches for the following discussion.

Formal refers to theological education in a formal, structured setting with the broad approval of church denominations or accrediting agencies, and it normally culminates in credentialing. This is also known as the traditional, conventional form, due to its systematic organization and formalized procedures in recruitment, content, objectives, and assessment. It leads to a qualification recognized by the relevant national educational qualifications framework. Large institutions, high costs, long procedures, and strict examinations are all characteristic of the formal. It is usually a registered, full-time residential, certification-oriented form of education, generally involving deeper cognitive

---

7. John Jusu, "Reflections of TEE from Overseas Council in Africa," in *TEE for the 21st Century*, eds. David Burke, Richard Brown, and Qaiser Julius, ICETE (Carlisle: Langham Global Library, 2021), 429.

capacities and a preparation for certain roles. Its goal is academic credentialing primarily focused on "knowing better." Its espoused values of the solidity of content and standardization of process sometimes appear to be the insubstantial aspects in the nonformal approach. FTE holds a unique place in the leadership and teaching functions in Christianity. Formal credentials continue to determine most strategic leadership positions in churches and mission organizations. It has also been noticed that the methodical learning style, substantial exploration of content, and broader worldview one gains through FTE provides the platform to speak and act for the renewal and integration of TE at large. Moreover, successful NFTE initiatives are said to be mostly led by those trained in FTE.[8] The strategizing and strengthening of NFTE are often viewed as stemming from the skills, competencies, and quality controls one gets acquainted with in the formal paradigm. At the same time, sharp criticism is raised among the churches and missions against traditional seminaries for being "ivory steeples" or "theological sausage machines."[9] The formal TE's structured classroom is judged for creating a dichotomy between theory and practice, thought and action, the sacred and the secular, and study and service.

Nonformal is tailor-made, usually short-term learning programs that meet the needs of learners in terms of skills development. Defining nonformal theological education has always been a difficult task. Not wholly willing to accept the term, many are looking for reasonable alternatives. It is neither an unplanned education open to all, nor a competitor to the functions of formal education. In 1999 Cannell asked,

> How do we provide theological education for the whole people of God?

---

8. Dallas Theological Seminary, "Training Pastors around the World: Michael A. Ortiz, Ramesh Richard and Darrell L. Bock," A dialogue over how TE is changing in and through the church, YouTube, 5 November 2021, https://www.youtube.com/watch?v=HVhF6khzNq4&t=219s. Also, Michael Ortiz, Ramesh Richard, and Qaiser Julius on ICETE live on Formal vs Non-Formal Theological Education, https://www.facebook.com/search/top/?q=ICETE%20live%20with%20 ramesh%20Richard, 4 June 2021.
9. Mike Starkey, "Ivory Steeples?," *Third Way*, October 1989, 22–24.

> How do we serve the continuing professional development needs of our alumni and other ministry professionals?
>
> What are the implications of conceiving of education not as preparation for some future ministry, but continuing development in ministry?
>
> How do we address issues of authority, power and elitism in higher education?[10]

Technically, "nonformal" represents any organized educational activity outside the established formal system – whether operating separately or as an important feature of some broader activity – that is intended to serve identifiable learning clienteles and learning objectives. It finds people on their life journeys, and addresses the questions and issues they are interested in, not necessarily leading to degrees or qualifications, but making relevant learning available in essential skill sets for life and service. The goal is to equip a person in context to "live and serve better." It offers educators the platform to attempt any method that works to train lives in families, churches, and societies. Ideally, NFTE is not an end in itself by developing skills in individuals; rather, it aspires to impact the shaping of the larger society with more trained people. Historically, it has served in training large numbers in mission and church planting by enhancing accessibility, educational inclusion, and personal empowerment by capacity-building.

> In 1972 the Theological Education Fund (TEF) enumerated several types or forms of alternative theological education: study centers, lay training institutes, centers for urban mission and training, theological education by extension, other decentralized programs, clinical pastoral education, community-based theological learning, cell groups for study, mutual care and team ministry, theological

---

10. Linda Cannell, "A Review of Literature on Distance Education," *Theological Education* 36, no. 1 (1999): 59–60.

reflection in liberation movements, and ad hoc educational events (workshops, conferences, short courses etc.).[11]

It might be significant that numbers are rising among the emerging leaders who upon graduation from FTE want to enroll in nonformal programs to fill the vacuums in calling, coaching, and capacities. For example, YWAM's (Youth With A Mission) Discipleship Training School (DTS) has theology graduates, after three to five years of formal TE, joining its programs for personal and missional formation. The nonformal paradigm addresses educational inequality in regions where the majority of leaders or believers have no access to training and mainstreams potential leaders who have been long hidden under the power-driven leadership structures. It helps by (1) *Encouraging people to learn*: With its innate flexibility in terms of prequalifications, capacity, time, and space, it invites people to keep learning. It gives hope that they can learn at their own personal level. How far the churches and missions are able to motivate their people to be learners is a critical issue, as decades can pass without any form of learning or refresher programs. (2) *Enabling the whole people of God*: NFTE enhances access to many who are denied a formal education opportunity. UNESCO 2010 held that nonformal education, with its scope of reachability and nondiscriminatory nature, provides a platform for individuals to grow and flourish at their own competency levels. This feature represents its vital importance for churches and missions, where the whole people of God need training and engagement. (3) *Enhancing willingness to take responsibility for growth*: Theoretically, NFTE does not relegate the learner to the receiving end; rather, it allows the learner to take prominence in the process. By facilitating immediate learning in context, rather than as an imaginary future move, it motivates persons to think and act. Through learners selecting resources, engaging in research, and creating ideas and outcomes, augmenting competencies to be a change catalyst is interwoven in NFTE's design.

Informal refers to the learning that happens naturally, all through life. The concept of informal learning was developed as early as the 1950s when Knowles wrote on "informal adult education." From its general educational connotation,

---

11. F. Ross Kinsler, "Theological Education by Extension: Equipping God's People for Ministry," in *Ministry by the People: Theological Education by Extension*, ed. F. Ross Kinsler (Maryknoll: Orbis, 1983), 1.

the term found significance later in the 1980s in human resource development that happens informally in workplaces. Informal is predominantly experiential, noninstitutional, unstructured, integrated with daily routines, and linked to the learning of others. Here learning happens informally in day-to-day life, from observation and participation, and from the unplanned and unintentional happenings all around. This is the way humans learn most things, acquire most skills, and acquaint themselves with new environments and challenges. When intentionally enhanced, it advances the growth of persons and thus becomes a core dimension of human learning and development. Research shows that as much as 70 percent of the acquisition of new knowledge and skills in the workplace occurs informally.[12] Conner wrote,

> Learning is continuous and all-encompassing, arising from everyday activities and events. Sometimes it is spontaneous; other times learners organize it as they do their work. It is not limited to a predefined body of knowledge (what is known) but instead emerges and is constructed from spontaneity and serendipity of personal interactions. It happens whenever and wherever people do their work; around a conference table, on site with customers, at a laboratory lunch, or on a shop floor.[13]

> Because informal and incidental learning are unstructured, it is easy to become trapped by blind spots about one's own needs, assumptions and values that influence the way people frame a situation, and by misperceptions about one's own responsibility when errors occur. When people learn in families, groups, workplaces or other social settings, their interpretation of a situation and consequent actions are highly influenced by social

---

12. L. Bruce, M. Aring, and B. Brand, "Informal Learning: The New Frontier of Employee & Organizational Development," *Economic Development Review* 15, no. 4 (1998): 12–18.

13. Marica Conner, "Informal Learning: Developing a Value for Discovery," in *Leading Organizational Learning: Harnessing the Power of Knowledge*, eds. Marshall Goldsmith, Howard Morgan, and Alexander J. Ogg (San Francisco: Jossey-Bass, 2004), 91.

and cultural norms of others. Yet people often do not deeply question their own or others' views.[14]

Being "unstructured" is both a strength and a weakness in a learning system. It is a strength in that it opens up the world of learning and allows flexibility and spontaneity, but it is a weakness because of the possible blind spots, lack of order, and misperceptions. A distinct feature of the informal approach is that individuals may not be highly conscious of their learning; yet, when they consciously allow space and focus for informal learning experiences, it liberates them to self-initiation and spontaneity, which are traits of deep learning.

Therefore, we should not substitute one approach with another, but recognize how in complementarity these three aspects can effect rich, transformative development in persons who are by nature unique in their capacities. Table 2.1 depicts the features that make each sector distinct. However, we recognize this polarity as a troubling reality that the theological education endeavor has been stuck with. Practical situations could be more fluid or overlapping than the table implies. The table presents some of the common ways of compartmentalizing, although there are always exceptions when it comes to holistic formation, quality assurance, and accreditation. For example, the ATA's (formal) accreditation manual strongly stresses holistic formation, and emphasizes responsive learning, reflective practice, and ministry skills development. Also, programs which some reckon nonformal, such as TEE programs, can be and are accredited formally. The determining factor for "formal" is primarily its recognition as a social, national qualification.

---

14. V. J. Marsick and K. Watkins, "Informal and Incidental Learning," in *The New Update on Adult Learning Theory: New Directions for Adult and Continuing Education*, ed. Sharan B. Merriam (San Francisco: Jossey-Bass, 2001), 31.

Table 2.1 Formal, Nonformal, and Informal Training Pathways

	Features	Formal (Academic)	Nonformal (Skills)	Informal (Life)
1	Type	Institution-based, 3–5 year time-bound, full-time, knowledge-focused, systematic, structured, assessed, certified	Skills and contextual needs-based, short-term, flexible, out of traditional academia, not always subject to external assessment or standardization	Unplanned, unstructured, natural learning in and through life
2	Center	Academic institution offers education that leads to a qualification recognized by relevant national educational qualifications frameworks	Individuals, specialized teams, Christian NGOs, mission organizations	No defined center, happens through all of life's experiences/situations
3	Learners	Knowledge-seekers, thinkers, entry with standard-level prior education, exit with degrees, aim higher education/leader roles	Skills/competency seekers, ministry practitioners, church members, less-structured prior education entry conditions, pre-experiences, achievements and contributions respected, exit may/may not be with certificates, expected to apply the learning into action	Every person, knowingly or unknowingly, no entry/exit points, natural way of gaining knowledge and skills
4	Formational Focus	Intellectual, cognitive pursuit, critical, analytical inquiry	Responsive learning, reflective practice, ministry engagement	Observation, imitation, paying attention, responding to mentoring or leading, self-improvement
5	Curriculum	Established, owned, and prescribed by institution, or designed and preserved by the faculty, externally approved for conventional academic standards	Designed or adapted to meet contextual needs and challenges, creating learning opportunities for those in and outside academia, innovating learning variety for better accessibility and feasibility	Unspecified

	Features	Formal (Academic)	Nonformal (Skills)	Informal (Life)
6	Modality	Campus-based or hybrid, with residential facilities, centralized and recognized standards	In-service/stay-in-community, online/blended, affords flexibility, self-defined quality expectations	Unspecified
7	Faculty	Scholars, academics, authors	Both practitioners and academics, reflective learning facilitators, pastors, mission leaders	Any person, situation, or experience at any point in life
8	Outcome	Defined cognitive outcomes, assessments, grade records, degrees, graduation, ministry/leadership positions, higher education paths	Outcomes assumed, sometimes specified, study period/contents not strictly imposed, learners attain desired skills to serve their contexts	Outcomes not established unless individuals do so by themselves
9	Potential Flaw	Ivory-tower image, banking model tendency, disconnect from church, less engaged in ground reality	Loose, unstructured, too liberalized, challenging traditional learning pathways, learners formed with little foundational knowledge	Undesirable experiences and environments produce unhealthy learning which is indiscriminately absorbed by individuals as lived realities
10	Public Approval	External agency accredits through standardized, recorded procedures, outcome socially recognized, transferable credits in wider academia	Specialized ministries or independent agencies may recognize/validate learning, social recognition by programs' contextual relevance or learners' achievements	The impact a person's life has on the well-being of closer communities and the larger society

The fluidity and complexity of the boundaries of these streams are demonstrated by Marvin Oxenham in his matrix approach,[15] relating theological education to academia, and not necessarily to the church. Much of the confusion emerges as different training networks use the terms "formal," "nonformal," and "informal" in different ways. For example, the

---

15. See Appendix 1.

Global Proclamation Commission network speaks of "formal" as theological education, "nonformal" as pastoral training, and "informal" as mentoring, with implicit definitions of what theological education is and is not, which poses questions for those who, like this present study, maintain the purpose to be the healthy building up of the whole people of God. Several training networks define theological education as exclusively for the formation of pastoral leaders.

The impacts, limits, and intersections of these learning forms have lately been dominating discourse in theological education, as in the ICETE global virtual consultations.[16]

Informal: Distinct Pathway or Undergirding Vitality?

There are training frameworks that hold "informal" to be a distinct sector with a standing of its own. The Global Training wing of the United World Mission (UWM) maintains that the programs train and multiply leaders for the church through the formal (comprehensive TE degree programs), the nonformal (scalable, practical training programs in person/online/hybrid), and the informal (ongoing holistic learning of believers and leaders). As noted above, the training framework of the Global Proclamation Commission,[17] with its motto "All pastor-leaders trained; every pastor a trainer," affirms that it trains through the defined streams of formal (theological education), nonformal (pastoral training), and informal (mentoring).

This approach of having "informal" as a separate category is not rare in missions that seek added emphasis on "ongoing pastoral mentoring and formation." For them, it is integral and, simultaneously, a specific pathway of authentic learning and growth.

However, by intention, the following sections will restrict the discussion to the formal and the nonformal types. The most widely accepted understanding of "informal" learning is that it happens all the time, wherever, whenever, so that in a formal, traditional setting, informal learning is the learning that results in the great power of the hidden curriculum. In this, learners informally observe

---

16. Forum threads from November 2021 to July 2022, "Formal and Non-formal Theological Education in Dialogue – C22," ICETE Academy, https://icete.academy/course/view.php?id=172.
17. Global Proclamation Commission for Trainers of Pastors, accessed 18 October 2022, https://gprocommission.org.

how their faculty or facilitators do things, how they relate to students and each other, what are credit-gaining elements and what are not, and so on. All this is informal learning. Informal learning is integral and happens all the time. When faculty put intentionality into harnessing this learning potential, it moves into the nonformal pathway. This makes its theorizing complex. Although "informal" assumes a central role in human learning and development, and is integral to the ongoing mentoring of leaders and pastors, this work holds that (1) it is not a structural continuum in education; (2) drawing its distinctions and assessment is different from doing so for the other two; (3) it often mutates and merges into formal and nonformal and the whole of life; and (4) it might be more reasonable to uphold its all-encompassing, all-undergirding role that impactfully underpins FTE-NFTE collaborative designs, rather than creating another pole of its own.

We will now discuss in detail the FTE-NFTE tension and its impact on ministry formation.

The FTE-NFTE Tension and the Impact on Ministry Formation

The class discrepancy in theological education between *established academic credentialing* and *ministry training credibility* has grown into polarities that have not served the training needs of the church very well. By overdoing cognition or practice, we often lack the holistic drive in education. Hough and Cobb diagnosed the malaise thus: "Theological education is torn between academic norms defined chiefly as excellence in the historical disciplines and modern professional norms defined in terms of excellence in performing the functions church leaders are expected to perform."[18] Farley critiques how the professional or clerical paradigm has shifted from its original intent: Personal formation drops out and becomes cocurricular; ecclesial integration drops out and theological education becomes more individualistic; sociopolitical and cultural standing is downplayed while common ecclesial commitment is lacking; and the bifurcation of theory and practice increases as seminaries tend to focus

---

18. Joseph C. Hough, Jr. and John B. Cobb, *Christian Identity and Theological Education* (Atlanta: Scholars, 1985).

on one at the expense of the other.[19] Wherever academia and ecclesia exist in tension, performative wholeness can be reached only through reciprocated strengthening, creative balance, and respectful and robust dialogue to gain valuable input from both. *Knowing, being,* and *serving* in Christian practice are aspects of one whole experience. Setting one against the others will cause us to fail in the purpose for our existence. For example, we should not be advocating for the "experiential" to replace the "cognitive," or vice versa; rather, we should explore models for meaningful interconnections for better synergy.

FTE and NFTE appear in many types and forms and they function on distinct values. Werner surveys the landscape of formal theological education, from smaller Bible colleges and training centers, to nondenominational theological seminaries, denominational theological colleges or seminaries, ecumenical seminaries, and national public universities with departments for religious studies.[20] NFTE forms include TEE, church-based cohorts or cell groups, short-term Bible studies (from three months to two years), short-term mission trainings, online or hybrid programs by seminaries, occasional courses by Christian NGOs, global online or extension programs, and more. There are characteristics that make NFTE particularly useful, such as accessibility, affordability, inclusivity, flexibility, contextual grounding or responsiveness, continuing learning, focus on competency, being tailor-made, problem- or need-based content, and more. While the academic and structural values of FTE are historically recognized, NFTE programs are regarded as serving alongside, filling gaps, addressing practical needs, and enhancing accessibility. What are the special features of NFTE? Do these value claims render to the NFTE programs a unique standing, to the extent that beyond serving alongside, NFTE can inform FTE and even contribute to it?

The need is for coached disciples, servant-leaders, holistically formed pastors, and practicing theological thinkers. The forms of training are changing as quickly as the sociopolitical realities are altering in this context. For instance,

---

19. Edward Farley, *Theologia: The Fragmentation and Unity of Theological Education* (Philadelphia: Fortress Press, 1983), 93–94. Also see Edward Farley, *The Fragility of Knowledge: Theological Education in the Church and University* (Philadelphia: Fortress, 1988).

20. Dietrich Werner, "Perspectives on the Future of Theological Education in Asia," in *Asian Handbook of Theological Education and Ecumenism*, eds. Hope Antone, Wati Longchar, et al. (Taiwan: PTCA, 2013), 659.

training expectations in certain places have changed from full-time to bi-vocational, drawing many more people into the service of the Lord. Women for whom ministry inclusion was only a mirage are being trained and are growing as ministry partners in closed and persecuted contexts, providing nonformal training for believers and missionaries. Studies have been published suggesting radical changes in the function and outcome of formal TE, challenging its siloed approach, elite orientation, and lack of ministry responsiveness. Simultaneously has come the serious caution, to those advocating a complete renouncing of FTE, against "throwing the baby out with the bathwater." In other words, whether keeping the baby in cold water, or throwing the baby out with the bathwater – either will have grave consequences.

Formal theological education in seminaries and Bible colleges is known to be the ideal platform for concrete theological formation, for comprehensive thinking, reflection, and response that underpins all dimensions of life and ministry. The danger is the "cathedral mentality" that increasingly detaches the learner from contextual and ecclesial engagement.

Criticisms against the rigidity of training forms have not been just a few. The World Missionary Conferences in Tambaram 1938[21] warned against theological education becoming the Cinderella of mission; Newbiggin termed the problem the "Babylonian captivity of theological education";[22] Athyal challenged irresponsive TE forms to stop being "prodigals doing their own thing";[23] and for Lloyd-Jones, theologians were becoming persons who knew nothing about how to handle people and often could not speak or preach in their language.[24]

Becoming an elite class that, consciously or otherwise, is separate from the church's "theologically illiterates" is directly termed by Heywood the "attitude of superiority."[25] Amid the complexities of social exclusion, chronic poverty,

---

21. Theological Education Fund, *Ministry in Context: The Third Mandate Programme of the Theological Education Fund (1970-1977)*, (Bromley: TEF, 1972), 31.

22. David Heywood quotes Newbiggin in "A New Paradigm for Theological Education?" *Anvil*, vol.17, no.1 (2000), 19.

23. Saphir Athyal, "Missiological Core of Theological Education, *UBS Journal*, vol.1, no.2, September (2003): 55.

24. Martyn Lloyd-Jones, *Training Men for the Ministry Today* (London: London Theological Seminary, 1983), 8.

25. David Heywood, "A New Paradigm for Theological Education?," *Anvil* 17, no. 1 (2000): 21.

persecution, and religious fanaticism in South Asia, theological grounding cannot be separated from the practical ministry of evangelism and church planting. This principle in training transcends countries and cultures. We need practical scholars who can answer worldwide questions in public theology and at the same time be reflective practitioners who live out their theological convictions in mission amid ongoing sociopolitical challenges. Interestingly, our training forms must integrate the elements of globalizing and localizing for lasting impact. Half a century ago, in 1974, Coe warned the Asian TE against developing a "cathedral mentality," pointing to the changing contextual needs:

> We must distinguish theological education, which is the ongoing process between the times, of the people of God in its pilgrimage, and the patterns of theological education which are, after all, the temporary tent-making process, changing from time to time though sometimes we are tempted to develop a "cathedral mentality" as if we were to be there forever.[26]

When the pathways of theological engagement and ministry engagement do not meet, it raises ultimate questions regarding training effectiveness.

When Knowledge and Practice Resist Meeting

Will these pathways meet? Can they meet? NFTE initiatives started functioning in parallel to seminary or Bible college education to meet the enormous ministry needs. Missions and churches were seeking to make Bible study accessible and comprehensible for their people and get them on the go in *doing* evangelism and church planting. As we noted in the previous chapter, research on the global church reports that nine in ten churches are led by pastors who do not have formal theological education. The contexts in South Asia where this statistic reflects the reality present us with the ultimate missional and leadership challenge. NFTE initiatives state the conviction that no single form of training can meet this mountainous need in the church. Hence TEE, distant, extension, and online programs, church-based Bible studies, seminar series,

---

26. Shoki Coe, "Theological Education: A Worldwide Perspective," *Theological Education*, Autumn, 1974, 7.

learning cohorts, and many more. Many of them intend their definition of success to reach beyond graduation, to lifelong learning that impacts the world with Christlike living and serving. That being said, we also recognize that the leaders and participants in the NFTE initiatives face unique challenges in educating people whose lived realities are characterized by unparalleled daily struggles for survival. Thus, quality assurance in the long run has become a concern for many given the lack of clear standards and learning assessments.

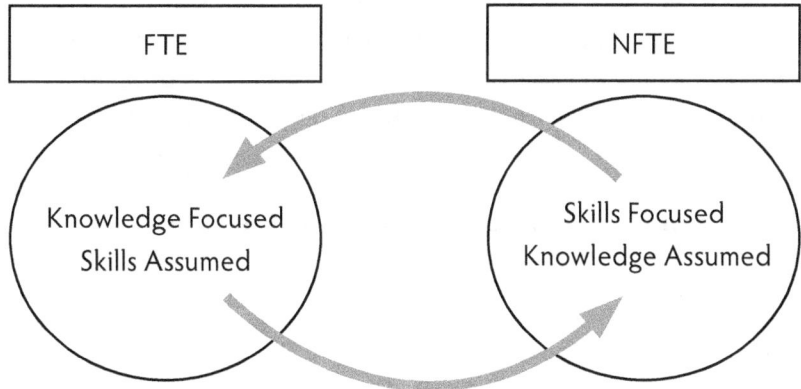

Figure 2.2 Making Knowledge and Practice Meet

Recent decades have witnessed a renewed awareness in South Asia of a holistic approach in training, contextualization of curriculum, tangibility of church-seminary relationships, and the critical role of NFTE initiatives in advancing mission and evangelism. Addressing church ministry formation in seminary education, Thomas formulated a Context-Based Transformative Learning Model (CBTL) in 2008 for formal TE settings to achieve more transformative missional impact.[27] Even so, he admitted that the seminary systems seemed too rigid or indifferent about revisiting their practices, while most of them preferred the convenience of embracing the narrow definition of TE as the dissemination of fixed amounts of information.

---

27. Jaison Thomas, "Church Ministry Formation in Theological Education" (PhD diss., Queen's University Belfast, 2008).

Tensions are real. Those upholding the case for FTE as having the central lead role ask, "If NFTE replaces FTE and FTE loses its ground, what will be the shape of the theological education enterprise in ten years?" The resounding fear may be one of losing the classical, historical foundation and direction of theological education. It could also be that when FTE's perceptible role in shielding from heresies fades away, the endeavor might over time reduce to an irredeemably complicated exercise. At the other end are voices saying, "How can FTE on its own meet the enormous need for training around the globe?" "When FTE continues to be inaccessible and unaffordable for the vast majority in contexts where Christianity is growing fast, what are realistic solutions if not NFTE?" Seminaries are doing great work, yet they are too limited to meet the enormous need for workers and leaders in the world today.

Table 2.3 outlines some of the common criticisms of both FTE and NFTE.

Table 2.3 Criticisms of Formal and Nonformal Theological Education

FTE Is Often Criticized for Being:	NFTE Is Often Criticized for Being:
Elitist	Poor in cognitive foundations
Exclusive	Disorganized in delivery patterns
Inaccessible	Overly flexible
Unaffordable	Unclear regarding pathway/s forward
Inflexible	Closed to other worldviews
Rigidly standardized	Incoherent in delivery
Overly abstract	Overly experiential & monocultural
Less communal	Flawed in assessment process

Most educators agreeing on the reality of the FTE-NFTE dichotomy also recognize that their distinctives have essential strengths in laying doctrinal and practical foundations in training. We know that theological education that is limited exclusively to the intellectual or practical realm would be dysfunctional. Generalizations such as "all FTE lacks spiritual/personal and ministry formation" or "all NFTE lacks academic formation" could be equally false; such conclusions would need to be tested against multiple factors. Effectiveness and ineffectiveness tend to overlap in training practices, and therefore it is unwise to make judgments based exclusively on the "method" and not on the "model" on which the method is used. For example, Banks's

Missional Model is built on certain erudite values: It is not a model bound by time or age, but a lifelong process whereby a person learns to live and serve in community; it comprehends the broader people of God and not just the elites; it orients itself primarily around "in-service" ministry activities; it can be done either in residence or by extension; and it should maintain a stronger connection between the seminary and the church and between study and practice.[28] Methods used in the framework of this model must correspond well with the model's philosophical grounding, to make learning and practice meet effectively. TE settings may tend to be inconsistent in resolutely putting the model into practice, or unable to do so. Doing so requires goal-setting, design, and intentionality.

Terminologies can imply polarities. For many, their first impression of the term "nonformal theological education" is something that is less authentic, less credible, nonacademic, nonprofessional, ad hoc. Nonetheless, until more inclusive and complementary vocabularies are jointly formulated, we are left with the terms "formal" and "nonformal." NFTE is often classified as diversified, extended, back-end, or tertiary education, and is criticized for democratizing TE and diminishing traditional TE structures. Academic systems tend to relegate NFTE programs to a lower status, as being at the margins and never at the core. The nonformal is seen as the handmaiden to ministry training within FTE or as a secondary, empirical aspect of theological education. Different vocabularies or analogies are used to signify the distinct practices of TE and to refer to the primary-secondary levels of professional formation. The "top rail" and "bottom rail," the "higher rung" and "lower rung," and the "helicopter hermeneutic" and "bullock-cart paradigm" may only intend to highlight the distinctiveness of the sectors, yet to many these are polarizing metaphors. Referring to the competing standards of excellence between academic credentialing and ministry training, Plueddemann wrote that these are "controlled by implicit values which are not open to dialogue."[29] In the ladder analogy, the higher rung signifies Level 3, the leaders, and the lower

---

28. Robert Banks, *Re-envisioning Theological Education: Exploring a Missional Alternative to Current Models* (Grand Rapids: Eerdmans, 1999), 144–47.

29. Jim E. Plueddemann, "The Challenge of Excellence in Theological Education," in *Excellence and Renewal: Goals for Accreditation of Theological Institutions*, ed. Robert L. Youngblood (Carlisle: Paternoster, 1989), 4.

rung, Level 1, which is "all believers." In most of the analogies in education, the highs denote the rational value at the top and the lows point to the practical or applied value at the bottom. Thus educating in ideas, absolutes, and theories is presumed to be of higher value and importance, while the contextual and practical are perceived as of secondary value. Within FTE-NFTE collaboration dialogues, this tendency toward degrading is a key aspect most NFTE leaders want to address. A primary need is to appreciate that the function of each is determined by the specific purpose and form of education it pledges to serve. On this basis, dialogue will be safeguarded from dwindling into debate as workable intersections for healthy associations will begin to be sensed. It is at this point that both can hopefully learn to make their distinctive features and contextual nuances known (without intimidation), examine reciprocity in collaboration, and benefit from cross-fertilization, concomitantly doing away with prescriptive standard-setting and/or claims to superiority.

Addressing the Dialectical Tension

An extensive amount of literature, and reports from consultations, dialogues, and commissions, has already been produced on this issue. Newer models have emerged, offering insights on the integration of learning in TE.[30]

Farley's Classical Model focused primarily on cognitive wisdom in theological education for the whole church. Hugh, Cobb, and Stackhouse introduced the Vocational Model, aiming at reflective and practical applications of Christian faith and its cognitive understanding. The Dialectical Model of Wood, Kelsey, and Chopp proposed to integrate vocational, social, mental, and behavioral with cognitive formation, while the Confessional Model of Schner and Muller focused on providing a systematic shape to Christian beliefs and direction for personal growth and the practice of ministry, holding cognitive and ethical insights. Banks's Missional Model emphasized that the whole church should engage in mission, calling for obedience in all the cognitive, practical, moral, and spiritual dimensions of the service of God's kingdom. The Formational Model was developed by Cheesman (Trinitarian), Lindbeck,

---

30. For a summary outline of the models with definitions, see Jessy Jaison, *Towards Vital Wholeness in Theological Education*, ICETE (Carlisle: Langham Global Library, 2017), 21–22.

and Tracy, focusing on spiritual and personal formation as key to TE, while Hall and Cheesman placed special emphasis on training as discipleship and mentoring. For Wheeler, it was a Contextual Model, and for Cannell, the focus was the church. Ferris, Conn, and Smith saw theological and practical wisdom as the unifying goal of TE, while for Collinson, making disciples as the prime directive of Jesus Christ should be the focal aim.

More practical efforts have emerged to meet the leadership and missional crises in the church. TEE was pioneered in 1963 at the Evangelical Presbyterian Seminary in Guatemala as a modest experiment and became a coherent extension program by 1966. It was birthed out of the conviction that "denominational residential seminaries were not serving the leadership training needs of rapidly growing churches."[31] The prototype was the result of addressing six issues which continue to characterize TE today.

> **Problem 1:** The numerical growth of the church led to the need for trained national leadership.
>
> **Problem 2:** Most of the graduates trained by the Seminary either never entered the specific ministry for which they were trained or else left it in order to enter non-church related occupations.
>
> **Problem 3:** The genuine leaders in the rural areas could not go even a few miles to attend a residential programme because of job and family responsibilities.
>
> **Problem 4:** "Take Home" studies used by the Extension students included lengthy reading assignments. These, however, were simply not being digested, especially by the less academically oriented rural students.
>
> **Problem 5:** Immense diversity in the educational and socio-economic levels of the students [was] evident. Persons of equally keen leadership and spiritual qualifications possessed radically different cultural heritages, social levels and academic backgrounds.

---

31. David Burke, Richard Brown, and Qaiser Julius, "Challenges Facing Contemporary Theological Education and the Case for TEE," in *TEE for the 21st Century*, eds. David Burke, Richard Brown, and Qaiser Julius, ICETE (Carlisle: Langham Global Library, 2021), 34.

> **Problem 6:** Particularly in the rural areas, many gifted leaders with innate intelligence had such meagre academic training that they could not even do the sixth-grade-level work required for the most basic courses.[32]

The Anglican Extension Seminary in Latin America began the project named Study by Extension for All Nations (SEAN) in 1971[33] and developed materials to resolve the ministry formation needs identified through careful inquiry. Samuel reports on TAFTEE in India using the SEAN materials in developing contextual learning materials.[34] Similar initiatives have sprouted up in many parts of the world genuinely aiming to bridge the training gap. However, in spite of the excellent materials and operational flexibility, extension programs have also encountered essential setbacks. The reasons for such impediments are, according to Hardy,

> when it does not fit locally, when many other similar programs are already there, when there is a lack of local ownership, when the costs for the entire endeavour in developing course materials, course mentors and facilitators were not counted, and when there is a lack of resources in the local languages.[35]

The ICETE Manifesto of 1981 highlighted the fostering of meaningful interconnectedness between all sectors and forms of theological education as one of its core values. The succinct statement said,

---

32. Kenneth B. Mulholland, "A Modest Experiment Becomes a Model for Change," in *Christianity and Education: Shaping Christian Thinking in Context*, eds. David Emmanuel Singh and Bernard C. Farr (Eugene: Wipf & Stock, 2011), 34–35.

33. Michael Crowley, "Study by Extension for All Nations," in *Ministry by the People*, ed. F. Ross Kinsler (Maryknoll: Orbis, 1983), 42. The name SEAN was taken from the third person plural of the present subjunctive of the Spanish verb "to be" found in 2 Timothy 2:2 where the instruction is given to Timothy to hand on the apostle's teaching to faithful people who will in turn be able to teach others. When there was an exponential increase in Protestant pastors who lacked formal theological education (only 20 percent had some form of FTE), SEAN came into being, addressing that need.

34. Vinay Samuel, "Globalization and Theological Education," in Singh and Farr, *Christianity and Education*, 87.

35. Steven A. Hardy, *Excellence in Theological Education: Effective Training for Church Leaders*, ICETE (Carlisle: Langham Global Library, 2016), 175.

We must embrace a greater flexibility in the educational *modes* by which we touch the various levels of leadership need, and not limit our approach to a single traditional or radical pattern. We must learn to employ, in practical combination with others, both residential and extension systems, both formal and non-formal styles, as well, for example, as short-term courses, workshops, evening classes, holiday institutes, in-service training, travelling seminars, refresher courses, and continuing education programmes. Only by such flexibility in our programmes can the church's full spectrum of leadership needs begin to be met, and we ourselves become true to our full mandate.[36]

The fifth ICETE consultation held in Cyprus in 1984 focused on "Theological Education by Extension (TEE) Come of Age," and the ninth consultation in Thailand in 1993 on "Affirming the Spectrum," all responding to the original declaration for interconnectedness. During the season of the COVID-19 pandemic, ICETE's virtual consultations made a momentous leap in welcoming and engaging all sectors of TE in strategic conversations for the future of the church. There have been significant attempts to renew the values and foundations of evangelical theological education and hence its unity of purpose. ICETE's Manifesto on the Renewal of Evangelical Theological Education in 1990 adopted twelve critical components for holistic TE, namely "Contextualization," "Churchward orientation," "Strategic flexibility," "Theological grounding," "Continuous assessment," "Community life," "Integrated programme," "Servant moulding," "Instructional variety," "A Christian mind," "Equipping for growth," and "Cooperation."[37] Unity of purpose and a sound biblical and educational underpinning characterize the manifesto. Even though this document has been grist for faculty discussion in many theology schools for a long time, Ferris points out the crucial role of educators in actualizing this, remarking, "Educators must tap their own

---

36. ICETE, "ICETE Manifesto on the Renewal of Evangelical Theological Education," accessed 17 August 2022, https://www.icete-edu.org/manifesto/html. (For the latest revised version, the "ICETE Manifesto II" (12 July 2022), visit https://icete.info/resources/manifesto/.)

37. ICETE, "Renewal of Evangelical Theological Education."

creativity to discern how advocated commitments can be implemented."[38] The Langham-ICETE literature partnership has impacted the integration momentum by promoting writings on theological education by writers from all TE sectors from around the globe. Such have become relevant platforms for multiple voices to be heard, even if for a time those voices might, to the traditional monocultural TE audience, sound less poised or polished. However, we also realize that contextual forms of learning or theologizing are often looked down on as exotic, lacking sophistication, or dealing with quaint issues of local interest. It may take time to overcome this by genuine collaborations that promote concomitant respect and sacrificial giving over of one's strengths for the betterment of the common vision. We maintain that change has to happen on the ground where life happens. "Change" or "shift" crafted and documented in the world events rarely get to impact the local settings.

The ICETE Manifesto II, the restatement in 2022, succinctly affirms the broader definition of theological education, stating that it is "beyond 'professional ministry' . . . beyond 'academic' . . . beyond 'formal.'"[39]

The Lausanne "Pastoral Trainers Declaration" stated,

> Since the formal and non-formal sectors of pastoral training have knowingly and unknowingly allowed ourselves to be divided in heart and efforts, we declare together that we shall endeavour to build trust, involve each other, and leverage the strengths of each sector to prepare maturing shepherds for the proclamation of God's Word and the building up of Christ's Church in all the nations of the world.[40]

The Cape Town Commitment states:

> A) Those of us who lead churches and mission agencies need to acknowledge that theological education is intrinsically missional.

---

38. Robert W. Ferris, "Accreditation," in *Evangelical Dictionary of World Missions*, ed. A. Scott Moreau (Grand Rapids: Baker, 2000), 33.

39. ICETE, "Manifesto II," 9–10.

40. "Pastoral Trainers Declaration" (Cape Town, South Africa, October 2010), https://rreach.org/wp-content/uploads/2017/05/Pastoral-Trainers-Declaration-Cape-Town-2010.pdf. See also Michael A. Ortiz, "ICETE Begins Year of Conversation on Relations between Formal and Non-formal Education," *Theological News* 51, no. 1 (Jan. 2022).

Those of us who provide theological education need to ensure that it is intentionally missional, since its place within the academy is not an end in itself, but to serve the mission of the Church in the world.

B) Theological education stands in partnership with all forms of missional engagement. We will encourage and support all who provide biblically-faithful theological education, formal and non-formal, at local, national, regional and international levels.

C) We urge that institutions and programmes of theological education conduct a "missional audit" of their curricula, structures and ethos, to ensure that they truly serve the needs and opportunities facing the Church in their cultures.

D) We long that all church planters and theological educators should place the Bible at the centre of their partnership, not just in doctrinal statements but in practice. Evangelists must use the Bible as the supreme source of the content and authority of their message. Theological educators must re-centre the study of the Bible as the core discipline in Christian theology, integrating and permeating all other fields of study and application. Above all theological education must serve to equip pastor-teachers for their prime responsibility of preaching and teaching the Bible.[41]

Wright affirmed,

The mission of the church on earth is to serve the mission of God, and the mission of theological education is to strengthen and accompany the mission of the church. Theological education serves *first* to train those who lead the church as pastor-teachers, equipping them to teach the truth of God's Word with faithfulness, relevance, and clarity; and *second*, to equip all God's people for the missional task of understanding and relevantly communicating

---

41. "4. Theological Education and Mission," in Lausanne Movement, "The Cape Town Commitment," section IIF, "Partnering in the Body of Christ for Unity in Mission" (2010), accessed 22 August 2022, https://lausanne.org/content/ctc/ctcommitment#capetown.

God's truth in every cultural context. Theological education engages in spiritual warfare, as "we demolish arguments and every pretension that sets itself up against the knowledge of God, and we take captive every thought to make it obedient to Christ." Those of us who lead churches and mission agencies need to acknowledge that *theological education is intrinsically missional. Those of us who provide theological education need to ensure that it is intentionally missional*, since its place within the academy is not an end in itself, but to serve the mission of the Church in the world.[42]

Following the formal education gathering of the ICETE Triennial 2015, an informal training consultation, the Leader Development Consultation (LDC), was held in Chiang Mai, Thailand, in 2017.[43] Through six case studies from Asia and the Middle East, LDC addressed a number of issues within Christian leader development in formal and nonformal trainings.[44] Several questions were addressed, including the following:

- What is happening that extends beyond or confuses traditional formal/nonformal definitions?
- How have these educational endeavors developed? What has been learned along the way? What might be the broader application?
- How can we see the work of Christian leadership development – in its broadest form – as encompassing many approaches that are complementary, at least potentially?
- How can all forms of leadership development become stronger and have greater impact?
- What is the starting point for conversations/forums of peer learning, cooperation, and experimentation?

---

42. Chris Wright, "Alertly Rooted! Energetically Engaged!" (keynote address, ICETE Triennial, Nairobi, 2012), quoting from 2 Cor 10:5.

43. Preceding dialogues started in 2014, as per the reports, where groups convened by Craig Parro, Riad Kassis, Jason Ferenczi, and David Baer began discussing points of intersection between formal and nonformal theological education. The distinguishing features of these dialogues were *listening to actual experiences of synergy* and *building relationships*. A group of fifteen met in Chicago in the fall of 2014, with a larger gathering of thirty in Antalya in the fall of 2015.

44. "Converging Streams? Thinking about Non-Formal and Formal Pastoral Formation in Dialogue," Leadership Development Consultation (LDC), Chiang Mai, Thailand, 24 May 2017.

This discussion will not do justice if we overlook the conscious efforts taken by formal TE institutions over the decades for self-renewal and transformation of their contents and delivery methods. Team teaching, faculty teaming up with students in ministry internships, informal Q&As outside classrooms, empirical, qualitative research projects, and incorporation of distance or extension programs are a few great examples. There are also instances where the nonformal programs provide more solid and sound content than the FTE. Blurred areas of overlapping strengths exist between the two. Accrediting agency Asia Theological Association (ATA), in its revised 2021 manual, expresses responsiveness to the collaboration of FTE and NFTE. The manual was credibly revised in 2016 and 2021 to endorse the value of whole-life discipleship, including skills, character, and relationships alongside the academic requirements as central to formal accreditation. Lua explains:

> We are committed to serve the formal and non-formal TE endeavours to do their best in the services for the Church. Obviously, ATA as a formal TE accrediting body has set a standard criterion for accreditation as any educational body, but we have provisions for equivalency assessments so that NFTE learners can avail [themselves] of accredited higher education if they want to. However, it is not the accrediting body that practically undertakes this procedure, rather, the local schools with whom the NFTE programs connect.[45]

With academic requirements being central to formal accreditation, ATA is aiming to find workable pathways to strengthen the training needs of the church through standard nonformal trainings.

An exclusive focus on pastoral trainers is the vision of the Global Proclamation Commission (GProCommission) that sets seven criteria for assessing pastoral ministry formation. The Bangkok congress discussed formal-nonformal reciprocity in depth and the report summarized that the task of contextualization in seminaries is not only in educational content but also in

---

45. Personal interview with Theresa Roco Lua, General Secretary, ATA, Houston, 28 July 2022.

pedagogy in non-Western contexts.[46] Formal institutions were encouraged to learn from the nonformal ones in this regard.

Re-Forma serves informal and nonformal training programs worldwide by providing a recognized global standard for outcome- and impact-based assessment. It provides thirty-five Standard Learning Outcomes – five major themes with seven subsets each – for biblical ministry training, primarily focusing on pastoral formation.[47]

Ample historical evidence demonstrates that solid thinking, consultations, and networking have gone into addressing the widening gap between academic and ministerial education. What our training enterprises lack is, perhaps, the clarity, consistency, and courage to innovate and lead the momentum in local contexts.

We need to be reminded that theological education is ministry itself; it is not a professional exercise outside of ministry. We often lose sight of that and tend to compartmentalize and complicate it with human philosophies and agendas. Making the parallel lines of formal and nonformal constructs meet may be hard but it is not impossible, while building relationships among people in both could be a fine prospect for the future of the church. TE as the forming of spiritual leaders and integral disciples requires a spiritual approach, as we see in the models of Jesus and Paul. Techniques, strategies, and planning certainly play significant roles in enhancing ministry, but they should not be ends in themselves. Theological education, and every kind of formation within it, is ministry; it is part of the process whereby God builds his kingdom and we as trainers, pastors, and teachers partner with him. More than professionalism, what brings it to fruition is our own lives lived as the hermeneutic of the gospel, incarnationally given away to reconcile a broken world to Christ. This implies more than systems, strategies, and infrastructures; it calls for ultimate dependency on God, yielding to the workings of the Holy Spirit, and selfless

---

46. Jonathan J. Armstrong, "Extending the Reach of the Traditional Seminary Classroom," Report of Session A, Open Dialogue Summary, the Global Proclamation Congress for Pastoral Trainers, Bangkok, Thailand, June, 2016. Revised Summary, September 2016.

47. Re-Forma, "Outcomes," accessed 24 August 2022, https://www.re-forma.global/outcomes. The thirty-five Outcomes are set under the five overall themes of "Knowing the Scriptures," "Living by faith," "Outreach," "Listening and Encouraging," and "Trustworthy Faith."

giving of oneself to the cause of the church and its mission in every stratum of society, just as the Lord Jesus Christ and the apostle Paul exemplified.

The following chapter presents the listening process undertaken as part of the research in this book. Listening to regional practitioners and leaders was a central task in the project, based on which the reenvisioning of training could take place.

The future is already here; it is just on the margins.
(Dave Gibbons)[48]

---

48. Quoted in Tod Bolsinger, *Canoeing the Mountains: Christian Leadership in Uncharted Territory* (US: Intervarsity Press, 2015), 189.

3

Listening Process 1: Lead Trainers/Faculty in Four Countries in South Asia

1. Listening Process 1: Opinionnaire 1: 32 lead trainers/faculty (LTF)
2. Listening Process 2: Opinionnaire 2: 10 regional training strategists (RTS)
3. Listening Process 3: Focus Group: 6 national catalysts/practitioners
4. Listening Process 4: Personal Interviews: 8 global TE leaders

Research Methods

For some, the formal and nonformal sectors are contradictory, while for others they run in parallel functioning distinctly to meet unique ends. A central mission of this project was to listen to contextual voices and envision responsive pathways for integrative theological education in the region's changing missional landscape. Listening to leaders and practitioners in four countries – Sri Lanka, Nepal, India, and Bangladesh – was with the intention of exploring the contextual feasibility of FTE-NFTE collaboration, toward assisting the church in its missional mandate. See Appendix 4 for Opinionnaires 1 and 2 Respondents' Details.

Given the time constraints of the project (five months), respondents from four countries for Opinionnaire 1 were selected through a "key contact" approach where a national leader from each country furnished a list of ten

TE leaders, each of whom could represent national voices with reasonable knowledge and experience across the TE spectrum. These are trainers with an average of twenty years of experience in training across the fields of both formal and nonformal TE. A total of thirty-two response sheets were collected. See Appendix 2 for Opinionnaire 1.

Opinionnaire 2 participants were purposively selected from the educational acquaintances of the writer to share their views from a regional perspective, on the grounds of their primary and long-term leadership in the field of TE in the region. Among them were premier thinkers in TE, acclaimed professors and writers, and those annually training several hundred. All ten key strategists responded. The intention was to make regional leaders speak in confidence about what they thought the problem was and how they thought it could be tackled. See Appendix 3 for Opinionnaire 2.

The focus group on Zoom was with six national TE catalysts, three selected from Opinionnaire 1 respondents and three young TE practitioners who were freshly invited to the process. The group discussed practical ways to address the polarities between training modes and the local church's ministry needs.

This was followed by a one-on-one conversation with global leaders in TE, eight of them selected purposively by the writer and interviewed individually via Zoom or in person. These are leaders of profound experience and a considerable level of influence in shaping deliberations on TE, and who could speak from a regional perspective. Each conversation lasted eighty to ninety minutes. The common themes running through the responses and the progressive clarity of perspectives helped in shaping ideas for further action.

The following sections present figures and percentages for a general visual representation of the data, which represent the number of respondents mentioned above. The percentage distribution in charts corresponds to the number of persons or the frequency of a theme in their responses. Open-ended questions sought descriptive feedback; manually done thematic analysis intended to capture layers of meaning in the data, if any. While the project would not aim at or claim generalizations from its observations, the four methods employed provide added confidence in presenting the South Asian voices. Data is presented in charts and direct quotes. To meet ethical commitments in ensuring confidentiality and protecting the identity of respondents, every name was assigned a code, in some cases both numerical and letter codes.

Listening Process 1: Lead Trainers/Faculty in Four Countries in South Asia 53

This chapter displays data from Opinionnaire 1, while the following chapter presents data from the other three stages of the listening process.

Listening Process 1: Opinionnaire 1: Lead Trainers and Faculty (LTF)

Respondents' Experience in TE

Respondents of the opinionnaires had a good knowledge of the context of theological education in their countries. LTF (Opinionnaire 1 respondents) had an average of twenty years of experience in theological education.

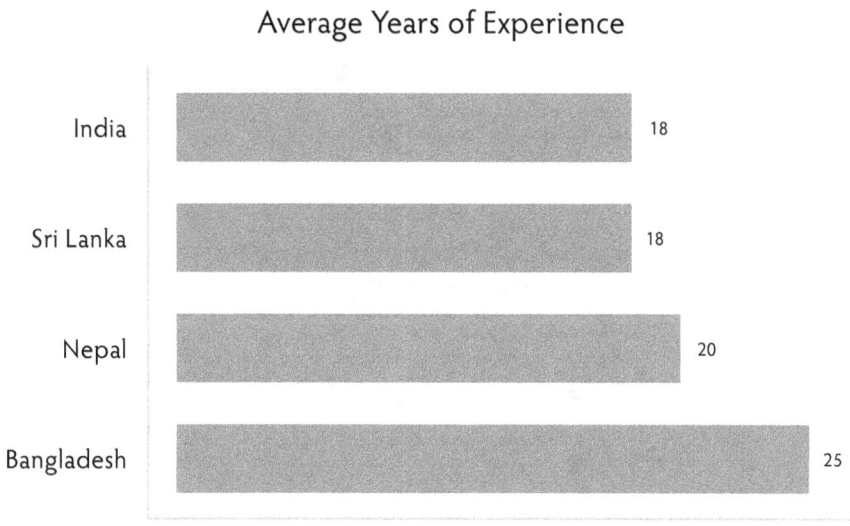

Figure 3.1 Lead Trainers/Faculty Experience in Theological Education

Student Distribution between NFTE and FTE

Figure 3.2 of the annual number of learners in the four countries in the ministries of the thirty-two respondents indicates that the difference between the formal and nonformal student numbers was immense. Although ideally FTE trains smaller numbers compared to NFTE, this chart implies the need for a greater collaboration between the two.

54 Building the Whole Church

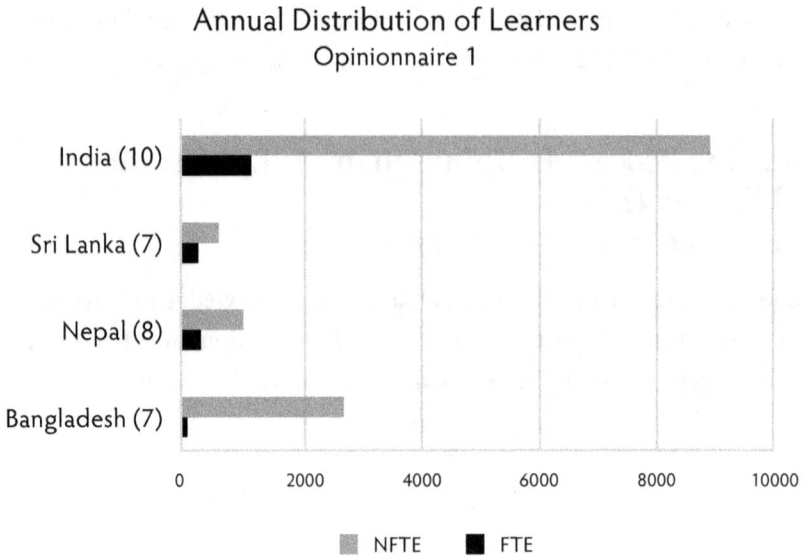

Figure 3.2 Student Distribution between NFTE and FTE

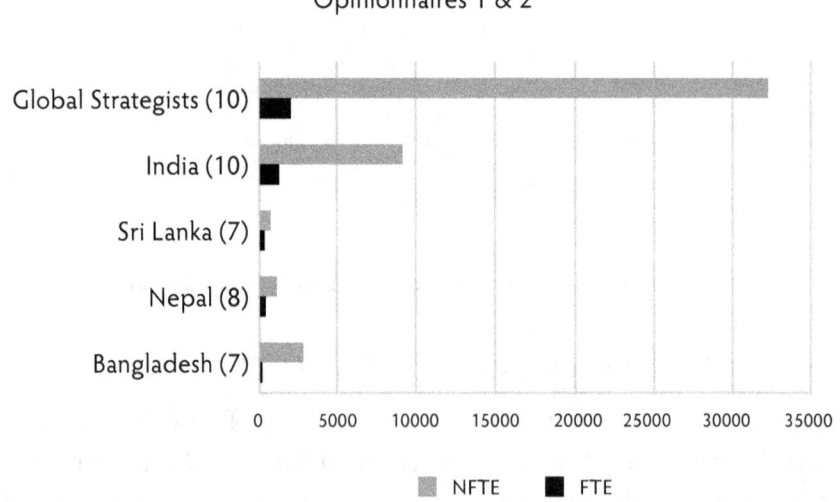

Figure 3.3 NFTE-FTE Distribution: Lead Trainers and Regional Strategists

FTE or NFTE Contributing to Church Planting/Growth in the Region

Forty-seven percent of responses from LTF showed that FTE and NFTE together contribute to church planting and growth initiatives across these four countries. While 38% specifically mentioned NFTE, 9% opined that church planting and growth happen solely by the efforts of the local church, while 6% pointed to FTE.

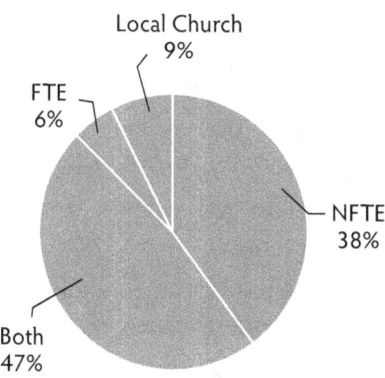

Figure 3.4 Training Mode Impacting Church Growth

Is the Estimate of 90% of Leaders Lacking Formal Training True in Context?

Eighty-one percent observed this lack as a reality in their ministry settings, while 19% of respondents disagreed. Responses varied within countries, as those who disagreed remarked that the figures depended largely on the urban/rural location of churches.

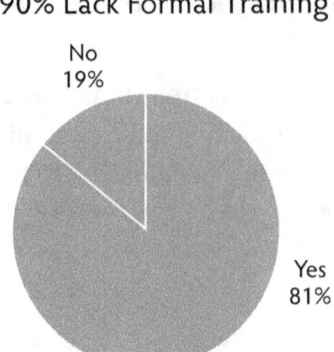

Figure 3.5 Leaders Lacking Formal Training

Major Concerns with Formal TE

Five major concerns were identified among the numerous ideas shared by respondents to Opinionnaire 1. Each classification contains several subcomments, while the single category with the highest number of comments was "Too costly." Respondents explained how hard it was for an ordinary person to leave family or church and pay for an education in a town. Bangladesh has only one accredited school while Nepal has ten schools with different programs accredited. India and Sri Lanka have a considerably stronger base of seminary education.

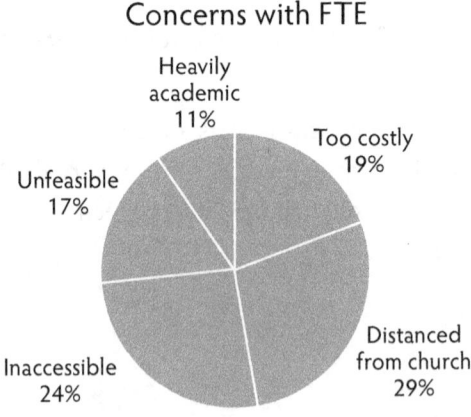

Figure 3.6 Concerns around Formal Seminary Education

"Too costly" was a stand-alone category.

The "Heavily academic" theme included comments such as the following: less spiritually enriching and heavily theoretical; creates a craving for individualistic learning rather than community-oriented learning and contribution; no concern for what the local community needs; and often provides only limited learning where there is no space to teach how to continue learning.

"Inaccessible" consisted of comments such as the following: there are only a few FTE accredited institutions in the country; high entry requirements; seminaries are situated in urban/semi-urban areas only; English language makes it inaccessible to most believers.

The "Unfeasible" category included the following statements: programs take too many years; falling (diminishing) social value/occupational value for seminary education; demands to be away from home and family responsibilities; constraints around poverty, age, and more.

"Distanced from the church" was presented by the respondents as a two-way reality; that is, the local church does not have a vision for proper theological education, and the seminary does not practically commit to a vision to provide training to serve the church. There were remarks that the church found FTE to be a waste of time; seminaries produced results that were not useful to the local functions of the church; local churches want trained workers, but they are not willing to invest financially or in any other way; seminaries need endorsements of students from the church, but are failing to shape those students for local ministry needs.

Some of the specific responses from Lead Trainers and Faculty on this issue were as follows:

LTF#19 "The church denomination I serve has around 90% trained informally by the church. My church has decided to train people within the church rather than send them off for long-term seminary education. It seems TE is losing its social and vocational value in my country."

LTF#10 "TE will not fulfill its role by training a few students in colleges; it must find ways to strengthen the body of Christ for the mission of God. This requires much commitment. Seminaries must take the initiative to work alongside the church and equip God's people for the work."

LTF#18 "The in-house seminary training is not attractive to our church. Senior pastors would not like their emerging juniors parting from church life for a number of years; they believe nothing can substitute for hands-on ministry education with direct teaching and leadership mentoring in the church. Our common complaint is that many faculty taught from their age-old notes without even suggesting methods to apply [their teaching]."

LTF#7 "I teach in a seminary and in nonformal education in my country. In the nonformal, I see a high motivation level in students. Oftentimes they do not feel academic pressure like in most conventional seminaries; rather, they choose it for some valid personal or ministerial reason. They do it thoughtfully and spontaneously. In nonformal learning settings, they seek answers for their deepest questions, they do a lot of searching in the Bible. Many of my seminary students grow as individually focused, profession-oriented persons, while in the nonformal, students passionately develop dynamic relationships to engage in ministry in their communities."

LTF#2 "Church often doesn't feel the compulsion for formal seminary education. [This] might be due to the small outcome or wrong outcomes. Church does not have the time, money, or manpower to provide its own training. This is the challenge."

LTF#3 "Character formation needs an organic, dynamic community. When a church is equipped to serve to this end, it becomes the best ground for this. Preparing the church toward this takes a value-driven vision and mission by which the church serves as the salt and light to the society we live in."

Every single remark around formal seminary education was analyzed and summarized under three overall issues, namely "Inaccessibility," "Heavily Academic," and "Distanced from the Church," as shown in figure 3.7.

Concerns with Formal FTE

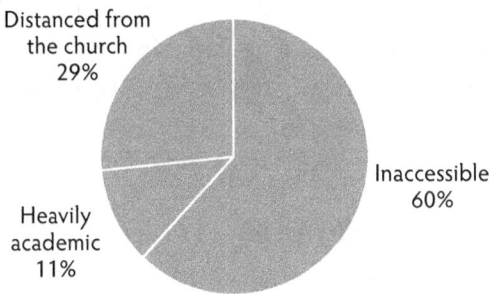

Figure 3.7 Summary Criticisms of FTE

Major Concerns with Nonformal TE

The main categories of concerns with NFTE derived from Opinionnaire 1 are shown in figure 3.8.

Concerns with NFTE

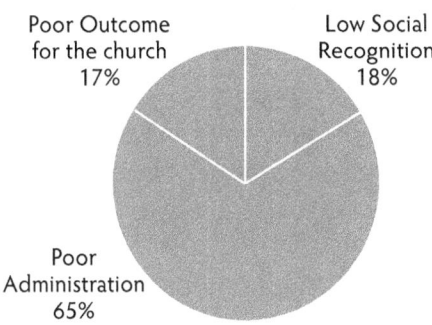

Figure 3.8 Concerns around Nonformal Theological Education

Responses under "Poor Outcome for the Church" included the following statements:

- "Half-knowledge causes the spread of wrong biblical interpretations and heresies."

- "When local language is not used, the impact on the student and the local community is small."
- "Anti-intellectualism is promoted, and after attending a short study program, people start doing things in their own way."
- "Large numbers on the entry list do not end up that way in finishing and serving their church."

Responses under "Low Social Recognition" included the following remarks:

- "Unaccredited programs are not so approved in the context."
- "Getting NFTE does not qualify persons for good leadership roles."
- "It is undervalued because it is different and something people are not used to; it does not have a ground for future growth of people."
- "Its rapid flourishing threatens the traditional seminaries, so it is kept away from greater social approval."

Comments in the "Poor Administration" category denoted functional issues in NFTE such as the following:

- "In my country, nonformal programs do exactly the same thing that seminaries do, in the same pedagogy and even in content."
- "These programs allow too easy entry and too flexible study plans which result in poor quality."
- "Everybody is in the same boat; little attention [is] given to learners' pre-skills/experience."
- "Deals with bulk numbers and no individual formation tracking."
- "Many programs get profit-oriented after some time, although they claim to be helping and serving the local people who have no other opportunity."
- "Big promises are made about learning at the beginning; but most of the time no one takes responsibility to deliver good programs. No follow-up on the students."
- "Little control, little follow-up on learning stages, little accountability, and little evaluation."
- "People get confused with occasional events with authentic educational programs."

The following is a selection of respondents' comments:

LTF#3 "Facilitators in NFTE tend to reproduce what they experienced in the traditional seminary classrooms. No wonder they dump heavy information in the form of printed learning materials, it's all they know. Facilitators need to be trained for their job, or we fail in the endeavor."

LTF#9 "We should not compare NFTE standards with FTE academic requirements. That is wrong. Evaluation in NFTE is based on the individual learner's goals and the local church's ministry purposes."

LTF#17 "In my context NFTE doing the same as FTE in content and process is very common, primarily because we have not developed creative educators who can make great designs and keep improving them. Any context-based learning must start with proper preknowledge/experience. Running programs with too many numbers without efficient tracking and individual student support is harmful to the entire field of education."

LTF#18 "Some NFTE programs run with a 'generating income mindset' with large numbers of learners enrolled. Rarely do these people know the learners well or even try to know their levels of spiritual maturity or learning capacity. In fact, good NFTE takes great effort, a careful growth-check, and efficient formational ideas."

LTF#4 "In my country, some of the NFTE make blind claims on the Holy Spirit and take learning easy and with no accountability. A careless selection of teachers ends up with a poor theological hermeneutic and haphazard learning. Many teachers do not want to stay on and they tend to be less prepared and more inclined toward the "food and fun" part of the sessions. With students lacking a learning pathway for the future and facilitators lacking proper payments (unlike their seminary counterparts), often the nonformal ends up as disintegrated, poorly coordinated occasional events."

LTF#27 "Church or seminary has nothing to do with many of the nonformal programs; its independent mold is a major issue in many places. When the nonformal programs fail to serve the learning needs of people where real life is happening, [NFTE] is not effective. Often these programs violate their own promises of skill-building and flexibility. Done hurriedly and carelessly, it makes for very poor outcomes."

Areas of Top Learning Needs in the Region

Respondents spoke for countries that have FTE and NFTE programs running at various levels. This question aimed to explore what their top areas of learning needs still are. "Discipleship" surfaced as a stand-alone need, while other thematic categories comprised multiple learning needs in the region.

For example, "Leadership" encompassed mentions of stewardship, servant leadership, administration, growth monitoring, and more. These aspects are supposedly already offered in the FTE/NFTE programs. If they are not, it would call for more details. We lack clarity on whether these topics are unavailable or not useful in the way they are currently offered. Why trainers/faculty remark on wide-ranging needs in leadership is a pointer for further probing, possibly in the advanced extensions of this project.

Comments on learning needs in the ministry context reflected respondents' concerns over the changing world and the ministerial challenges it raises; for example, several comments mentioned "today," "today's world," and so on. Local fundraising methods, shame culture and ministry, next-generation leadership, children's ministry today, discipleship in today's world, connecting with majority faiths in today's context, understanding Christian history in today's world, and minority rights are examples of needs in the subcategories pointing to choices for context-specific, time-sensitive, and responsive education.

Figure 3.9 Dimensions of Major Training Needs

Strengths of FTE and NFTE

All through the listening process, respondents randomly commented on the strengths of the formal and nonformal training patterns. A summary of their remarks in table 3.10 will help us see what trainers/faculty identify as ideal about these sectors. The figure represents highlights extracted from Opinionnaire 1.

Table 3.10 Strengths of Formal and Nonformal Modalities

IDEAL FEATURES: FTE	IDEAL FEATURES: NFTE
Disciplined, standardized structure	Design variety offers flexibility and inclusivity
Social recognition	Strong focus on Bible and methods of Jesus
Educational continuum	Learner-oriented (not system-oriented)
Broader placement possibilities	Assists church and responds to the needs of believers
Theoretical confidence	Holistic training design
Thinking skills	Practical, hands-on focus
Further education pathways	Improves and develops quality of life and service
Structured exams and evaluations	Equitable scope for formative assessment
Reading and writing skills	Continuing learning to both the learned and the marginalized
Leadership roles in churches/organizations	Need-based and contextually relevant approach

Will FTE-NFTE Collaboration Do Good in the Context of Training?

A majority (84%) responded positively to the idea of formal-nonformal collaboration. However, everyone added some restraints and concerns about the prospect. It was evident that while theoretically they appreciate the idea, they assume it will be challenging or impossible to practice in their training contexts. The specifics of this are covered in the section below titled "Concerns over FTE-NFTE Collaboration."

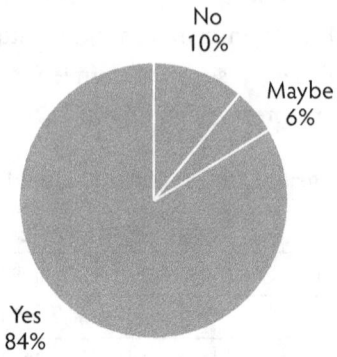

Opinion on FTE–NFTE Colaboration

Figure 3.11 Opinions on Formal-Nonformal TE Collaboration

Those who responded "No" explained why they were apprehensive of collaboration in their context.

LTF#18 "The systems they operate in are different. It is a power battle for FTE who will be losing control and an identity crisis for NFTE whose values will need to shift. The desire and willingness for such collaboration in my country is very little or nil."

LTF#32 "Standards, goals, and qualification requirements are different and, in most cases, uncompromisable. Expectations of cognitive and practical competences vary greatly in both. Finally, NFTE will have pressure to be turned into FTE."

The respondents checking "Maybe" shared their hope for collaboration but simultaneously expressed the practical difficulty in achieving it.

LTF#17 "Real tension exists due to the stronger social value of FTE and poor recognition of NFTE. This is not easy to resolve, it is a deep-rooted mindset."

LTF#12 "Maybe a brand-new strategy will help. If collaboration is not genuine, it will produce more confusion, institutional-level abuse, and conflict, which will damage the mission outlook in the country."

Concerns over FTE-NFTE Collaboration

There were detailed observations and opinions regarding this matter. The major concerns which emerged on issues relating to FTE-NFTE collaboration were as follows:

- Denominational controls and donor preferences
- Fundamental structural distinctions
- "Better be separate" attitude
- Institutional status quo
- Utilitarian, selfish mindset
- Cognitive competence disparity
- Unwillingness to admit the strengths of the other
- Labelling NFTE solely as a grassroots training endeavor
- Strong stereotypes in society and church
- Lack of awareness of NFTE pathways in secular education
- Poor vision on being responsive to changing needs/trends
- Driving forces of money, power, external controls
- Lack of creative thinking and networks

The following are a few concerns raised in comments by the respondents on the issues in FTE-NFTE collaboration in their ministries:

LTF#3 "FTE by nature cannot recognize the value of impact of NFTE, so it is closed for any concrete association unless for its own benefit. While FTE fears losing power, NFTE fears being transparent about its form of education."

LTF#5 "Collaboration might take away NFTE's opportunity in equipping many people in the church who otherwise have no chance for learning."

LTF#7 "Two systems that are very different cannot collaborate; it may be better for them to be separate in their functions. It is the way things have always been. Everyone knows the good things collaboration can bring; yet no one considers a strategy beyond the traditions. Walls are iron-strong."

LTF#8 "Depending on donors' interests, denominational preferences and policies, and our continuing dependency on external resources, collaboration of FTE and NFTE does not seem workable in our context."

LTF#12 "[Collaboration] will only collapse everything; a strict and a flexible curriculum will not work on the campus at the same time. Also, the funding (or financial matters) methods are very different in each; this will have impact at the organizational level of administration."

LTF#13 "Persons with lesser prequalifications will be undermined in a collaborative frame, their trainers too. Better avoid the chance of such humiliations."

LTF#22 "When these two types collaborate, certifications will not have clear meanings."

LTF#23 "Without FTE the overall knowledge base for Christianity will be weakened."

Methods of Collaboration

Comments generally called for more discussions, conversations, listening, and learning around the actual needs and strengths of each party:

LTF#9 "It sounds good, but very difficult in practice. For viable collaboration we need a uniting vision that makes sense to people and helps them find meaning and passion to work for. Other agendas operate normally on egoistic notions and end up in internal conflicts. We need a reason that will serve the eternal purpose or value of God's kingdom."

LTF#10 "Collaboration is good but will work only with a uniting strategy. In any case, it requires humility and a real willingness for sacrificial sharing. Such level of intentionality comes only with a vision that drives beyond our present institutional parameters."

LTF#11 "What will help is a 'no duplication' policy along with a compelling, uniting vision. Both must be ready to share resources including infrastructures, learning resources, and teachers."

LTF#16 "Will churches be upfront about initiating collaborations? Otherwise, the two conflicting sectors will only end up in even more trouble."

LTF#17 "Our country is facing challenges of constant splitting of churches and rapid spread of heresies. The church needs to shift its mindset from being so overly inward-looking, managing only the internal and infrastructure matters. There is a greater call on the church. When it neglects and passes on its prime responsibilities to parachurch organizations, it loses its life and existence."

LTF#19 "There are pathways developed by governments' tertiary and vocational educational commissions to qualify nonformal learners. With preknowledge, experience, and portfolios of contributions they are given pathways to reach up to the highest level of formal degrees."

LTF#24 "Usually FTE is seen as the sole resource base for NFTE or others; this attitude makes NFTE lose its identity when it comes to collaboration. There is so much NFTE can contribute. For some reason, NFTE leaders hold back, maybe lacking confidence. FTE on its own can never meet the enormous needs in the mission and leadership development of the church."

LTF#26 "Collaboration is good if each one recognizes the need for the other, each one willing to be at the same table with equal dignity and worth in their own style, and each abstaining from prescribing to or undermining the other. It is good to dream that this will happen one day."

LTF#6 "Many institutions try collaboration with a one-time resolve. Once a decision is made, they leave it to work on its own efficiency. Theological or ministerial education in complex sociopolitical contexts needs collaborative patterns that have geographical and locale-wise relevance. This should be a collaboration of visionary trainers who innovate and improve methods of sharing ideas and capacities."

LTF#28 "For good collaborations to be birthed and sustained we need detailed discussions on the needs, trainers' training, and goals. Clear understanding of funding policies is crucial in the long run. We must keep evaluating the tangible outcomes of our training in villages and cities and move forward improving the approaches."

LTF#29 "Church should be at the core of plans and strategies. There is a big disconnect where only the church can fully know what learning is needed and what process will make it happen where it exists. There is much more listening needed among us."

In Listening Process 1, responses on methods of collaboration of churches, seminaries, and mission organizations highlighted the need for three primary foci:

1. The need to discuss, listen, and learn deeply
2. The need for a uniting, compelling vision
3. The need to have the church and its mission at the center

Several of the respondents commented on the seminary initiating the collaborative efforts, but none expressed confidence about the prospect of a true and healthy interaction of FTE and NFTE. There were suggestions that the efforts must go slowly, based on study and deliberations. It was recommended that the agenda of collaboration should not lead to further gaps within training but be thoughtfully tried in situations where the value, purpose, and practice of each stream of training is regarded.

Dimensions of Quality Assurance for NFTE Initiatives

Opinions on quality assurance for NFTE initiatives offered profound observations, mostly corresponding to the philosophy of holistic education. These ranged from *knowing the learner well* to *evaluating for improvement*. The following points are taken from comments on quality components in nonformal TE as viewed by respondents. Numbers marked in brackets at the end of comments indicate the occurrences of mentions.

Solid Design

- Start from a good ground research.
- Education must reach beyond reading materials and occasional lecturing.
- A reasonable structure for the learning process is necessary.
- Have a clear statement of goals and specific plans to reach them.
- Good knowledge of the city, and of rural-urban distinctions in training, is key.
- Start with a short-term sample, learning of the needs, and make continuous improvements with the help of learners.
- Work out a standard nonformal curriculum that is holistic and presentable to any educator.
- There should be a learning track, evaluation, mentoring, and a motivation plan for each learner.
- Quality is about being Christ-centered, mission-driven, Bible-based, and church-supporting.
- Keep comparing course content and people's knowledge needs and problems. [3]
- Solid grounding on the Bible, and the overview of the Bible story, must be integrated in every aspect. [4]
- Training should be available for everyone.
- Knowing the levels of biblical literacy and comprehension of the learner is important.
- Meaningful designs must be made for learning assignments and their proper evaluation.
- Know the prospective learners well: their experience in Christian faith, giftings, and goals. [4]

Administration/Facilitation

- Develop thoughtful criteria for learners to be equipped in personal life and ministry. [3]
- Build a consistent rapport with leaders of churches, NGOs, mission organizations, and seminaries.
- Develop a wise funding base for continuity of the program; do not stop in the middle.
- Administrators and facilitators must be trained to be consistent, serious, and responsible in their service. Do not engage teachers who teach made-up stories, unbiblical content, and heresies. [4]
- The administration team must go beyond technical arrangements to oversee effectiveness.
- Wider consulting with educational experts and continuous listening to local leaders will help greatly.
- Facilitators must be experienced in theological education and active in practical ministry.
- Some form of recognition and certification according to learning stages needs to be given. [2]
- Learning in the vernacular and learning from experienced local leaders/pastors will make a difference.
- A relational and incarnational approach should be promoted.

In-Ministry and Interactive Learning

- Ministry engagement must be real, not imaginary or for requirements' sake. [5]
- Ministry or leadership opportunities (small or big) must be provided for all learners.
- Introduce learners to different models of leadership and ministry.
- Innovate with local languages, orality, creative art, and cultural learning styles.
- Have a reasonable time of residential learning.
- Deep experiences of prayer, Scripture meditation, and worship must develop in the learner.
- The program must be based in a community for participatory learning and group feedback. [4]

- Quality interactive sessions with practitioners and theologians will transform lives.
- The learning pattern should move people from a personal/institutional agenda to serve the church/mission. [2]
- Group interaction and discussions with peers must be accompanied by reviews for improvement. [2]

Follow-Up and Evaluation

- Ongoing evaluation of how much the learner grasps is important. [3]
- A proper layout of quality stages and competency stages should be created.
- Learners must be helped to apply their learning; provide them with guidance and opportunities.
- Formulate various methods for accountability and integrity in life and learning.
- Evaluate and improve methods from time to time. [3]
- A common coaching base for facilitators will help them grow and enhance the quality of the program. [4]
- Quality nonformal education is not too complex; it is practical and biblical. [2]

Table 3.12 Enhancing Quality in NFTE

Summary Points
Know the learner
Capture church's needs
Coach the facilitators
Let Bible be the foundation
Grow in relational mentoring
Apply learning variety
Listen to local leaders
Use vernacular
Apply learning variety
Think all levels
Design group interactions

Consult other educators
Keep administrators accountable
Build rapport with local churches
Provide real ministry engagement
Put them in leadership tasks
Plan wise funding for continuity
Innovate learning assignments
Evaluate for improvement
See geographical learning distinctions
Be Missionally-Driven
Stay centered on Christ
Be grounded on the Bible
Do it all to build the church

Opinionnaire 1 respondents made several recommendations for quality assurance in nonformal programs. The following are a few quotes.

LTF#22 "Leaders and facilitators of NFTE need to know learners' motivations and interest levels, their knowledge and resources they use, their experience in Christian faith, and their gifts and goals. It is a relational form of training persons in their communities. It is incarnational and deeply formational if designed and applied with intention."

LTF#6 "Learners must get in through specific criteria as relevant to the variety and flexibility of NFTE. It is important for them to realize this is not an easy/relaxing shortcut education, but rather a profound training opportunity they are accountable for. To ensure this, first the program admins and facilitators need to be coached well."

LTF#1 "Residential experience for whichever period is viable for the learners must be integrated in the design. To lift their confidence, and provide quality interactions with practitioners and theologians and marketplace evangelists, they must be taken beyond mere reading of materials and attending lectures in contact sessions."

LTF#31 "Training is needed for all and at all levels. Identifying the levels of thinking and biblical literacy is key in determining the quality of the learning design."

LTF#15 "NFTE is not about too much knowledge accumulation. It should be practical, participatory, strongly rooted in the Bible, and founded on central theological truths, which are simple, not complicated arguments."

Worth mentioning here is the document produced by the ICETE's track on "Relevant Quality Assurance by and for NFTE" from C-22 in Turkey, titled "Characteristics of Effective and Fruitful Nonformal Theological Education."[1]

Analysis Summary

1. NFTE is a tangible presence in South Asia in varied forms and at various levels. Even without considerable socio-ecclesial recognition it makes an explicitly greater presence in terms of student enrolment.
2. Both FTE and NFTE present great strengths and serious flaws, and they represent solid standpoints in their own values and purposes.
3. Educators and trainers are appreciative of the prospect of FTE-NFTE collaboration but simultaneously express their apprehension about legitimately complementing, and equally foregoing, practices in their contexts of ministry.
4. Despite the numbers of available FTE-NFTE programs, leaders point to significant learning needs in the region for the healthy growth of the church in changing times.
5. Quality is to be defined by the goals set and the approaches followed. Serving unique goals, FTE and NFTE follow different approaches, and hence quality definition and assurance cannot be single-track.
6. Defining and developing quality indicators for multilevel NFTE might be demanding, but nevertheless are still necessary.

---

1. ICETE, "Characteristics of Effective and Fruitful Nonformal Theological Education" (April 2023), accessed 18 May 2023, http://icete.info/wp-content/uploads/2023/04/Characteristics-of-effective-and-fruitful-nonformal-theological-education.pdf.

4

Listening Processes 2-4: Global, Regional and National Voices

Listening Process 2: Opinionnaire 2: Regional Training Strategists (RTS)

Opinionnaire 2 was the tool for the second stage of the listening process. The ten TE strategists with an active regional contribution in South Asia responded with an average of twenty-eight years each of training experience. While responses from the LTF focused primarily on identifying and explaining practical concerns, the RTS respondents pointed further to some core issues and their views regarding the way forward. Due to the significance of the detail in their responses, data is mostly presented in quotes as received, with removal of any names or other specifics that would be identity-revealing.

Views on Accreditation of NFTE Programs

RTS/HX "Accreditation procedures in the traditional way will turn NFTE into FTE. Thereafter new forms of nonformal will emerge, and that will add tension to proximate forms of FTE."

RTS/GW "Formal accreditation criteria obviously have little room for the nonformal type of education, simply because they are shaped for a distinct purpose. Requirements on the size of library collections, faculty qualifications, publications, facilities, infrastructures, and economic security are neither possible for nor relevant to other forms of education. The constituencies NFTE serves are mostly those with limited or little access to seminary education or even formal schooling. If learners still produce greater outcomes and exhibit competency in serving the local needs, maybe we need to redefine the process of recognition or accreditation. Whose need? Whose agenda? How to discuss? What to achieve? – there are several questions to tackle."

RTS/AQ "The two types cannot be put under the same sort of evaluation or standardization process. Doing that will make one lose its identity and contribution. Moreover, the nonformal stream is too diverse for a single formula of evaluation. I think a distinct and detailed planning would be necessary to set out multiple plans for validation (not exactly accreditation) for various levels of NFTE initiatives, laying out pathways for any level of education for those seeking them. The secular education field has a lot to teach us in this regard."

RTS/IY "Even the question of accreditation must be addressed with the church at the center of our discussion. We have compartmentalized TE to the extent that the church is nowhere on the scene while our systems turn more and more into dialoguing over technicalities and technologies."

RTS/JZ "There is a strong value given to formal education in the secular Asian context, but the nonformal is officially unrecognized, thus a tension is ongoing. I am not sure if we can resolve this tension in our context. It depends on the criteria we use to measure FTE and whether the same criteria could be used for accrediting NFTE."

RTS/CS "If the formal accreditation is assumed from the following sequence: Accrediting Agency – Accredited Institution (theological seminaries, not the church) – Trainee, then a proper accreditation may resolve the tension. But if the validation process is to support the mission and ministry of the church, then the priority given in the sequence would then be Church – Trainee – Accrediting Institution/Trainer – Accrediting Agency; we may have to work out an alternative system of validation."

RTS/FV "Regarding the question of accreditation, there are many profound and foundational issues that need to be addressed."

RTS/EU "Instead of thinking of new accreditation paths and new institutional alliances, we must come around the table to revisit the biblical and historical mandate for us as teachers and trainers. In fact, the matter of our concern should not be FTE or NFTE or accreditation, but the church. The Bible has taught us about the birth, life, teachings, death, and resurrection of Jesus, the Great Commission, and the church's mission in the world. This is a straightforward and convincing scheme around which the entire history of the

Bible stands. One thing that we may need to pledge together as leaders is not to further complicate the discussions. It is time to serve the church, which in my opinion is and should be the agent of theology and training."

RTS/BR "Formal and nonformal cannot come on par in South Asian minds. Efforts to accredit the nonformal are therefore likely to result in them adapting what the formal sector is doing, missing out on their own purpose and contribution."

RTS/DT "There are different sources of tension. Formal accreditation may resolve some of these, but not all.

"I think it's helpful to limit the term 'accreditation' to formal programs. Accreditation has the word 'credit' embedded within it. It's a word that belongs in the formal, credit-counting domain. If so, whenever an NFTE program is successful in gaining accreditation, it has, by definition, entered the formal world, and yes, the tension is then resolved. It has been resolved by changing the status of the program from 'nonformal' to 'formal.' And there are many currently nonformal programs which would aspire to develop in this way. In this case, formal accreditation resolves the tension. There's a middle way that is strongly encouraged in secular education worldwide. This is the process of assessing the formal 'cash value' of the nonformal education received. But many – perhaps most – nonformal programs do not want to seek accreditation, with the many requirements involved in their context, and perhaps a formal accreditation system is based on different values. Two suggestions for resolving the tension arise: First, the tension can be resolved as people meet and understand one another and recognize that they are working together for the glory of God, and for the equipping of the people of God for the mission of God. Second, instead of accreditation, quality assurance may help."

Summary: The responses denote that the formal manner of the accrediting process does not seem to help or point the way forward for nonformal education programs. The felt need is for more discussions and concrete thinking about ways in which NFTE programs could be recognized, validated, or quality assured. However, while deliberating on such matters, educators and systems focus more on technicalities and less on the church, as the responses indicate. It was implied that the consideration of quality assurance for NFTE needs to consider the frame of its church/mission-ward goal. Its methodological variety is central to its goal, and deeper deliberations on the same were recommended to prompt the momentum to continue.

Methods of Validation or Quality Assurance (QA) for NFTE

RTS/GW "NFTE's validation must be based on what it aims to achieve and how it has prepared a learning track for that. NFTE forms are too diverse to be brought under a common guideline, but general expectations may be laid out. This should not be shaped outside of the church, but rather by keeping the church at the center of the discussion."

RTS/FV "There are national Christian councils and alliances that may recognize the work of a member institution or church body offering nonformal training. Such umbrella networks that function as affirming partners of national/international recognition can offer effective validation without insisting that the NFTE must have the characteristics of FTE. Not all 'education' is made effective by formal accreditation criteria; in fact, forcing a formal model on some forms of NFTE will be a sure way to undermine their effectiveness. NFTE must be encouraged to articulate a transparent mission statement, a clear educational philosophy, and an assurance of what it undertakes to fulfil."

RTS/AQ "There could be some standards for quality assurance for NFTE. Today we see more accrediting organizations emerging that accredit the existing accrediting organizations. There are more complexities in academia. The system of education is becoming more complicated, ending up with efforts that ultimately do not count for anything significant in the growth of Christianity . . . NFTE cannot be evaluated with the same measures as FTE; its contextual dynamics are too diverse to be boxed in. An overall frame of validation must be developed through deep listening and dialogue among all parties."

RTS/EU "Criteria for validation must avoid unnecessary technicalities and confusion. Starting with knowing the learner's spiritual and intellectual maturity and will is important. Quality assuring procedures need to start with the student's biblical knowledge, commitment to life and ministry calling, attitude to work and leadership, recognition by the community, giftedness and teachability, and so on. QA and validation have too many dimensions needing much learning."

RTS/DT "A training's validation can be done based on transformed lives and the effective ministries of those who are trained. This is true whether it is formal or nonformal. First, the design must be evaluated. Second, the process itself must be evaluated while the training is being done. This must be constantly evaluated and improved. Third, the fruit of the training must be evaluated – over the long term. There are really three main goals for the work: transformation in the lives of those trained; increase in their effectiveness in their ministries; and their vision and capacity to build more persons."

RTS/CS "We should have some system to evaluate the output of an NFTE initiative over the past several years as part of the quality assuring process. Solely on the grounds of occasional activities, no program should be validated. Expectations of the learner must be made known and they must be presented for an appropriate method of evaluation. If it achieves the goal of ministry and personal formation, it must be validated by the criteria set."

RTS/JZ "The church(es) in the region has a vital role to play in recognizing and encouraging quality in the programs that seek to serve it. Quality will be discovered in relation to the church(es) in the context. How does the program seek to serve the church(es)? What is the experience of the church(es)? Can these programs work with the church(es) to agree on what quality means for the church(es)? I think this is one of the foundation processes for NFTE quality assurance. There are two tasks. One is more with those in formal education who want to build bridges between their formal world and the nonformal programs around them. A bridge must reach both ends, but the requirements of the formal world are usually defined by the secular educational system of the country. The other task is a quality assurance process that seeks to serve NFTE on its own terms, without reference to the formal world – helping NFTE programs to do what they are called to do, fruitfully and well. In this second task, 'steps of quality assurance' may be a healthier way of speaking about QA for NFTE than 'standards.' If NFTE can develop ways of talking about QA that are distinct from FTE accreditation, that will be helpful for this task. The groundwork will be to seek to establish values that are important for NFTE practitioners. What matters to the people involved? The steps/quality indicators must grow out of these values. There will be a range of values, and a range of quality indicators. I suggest there should be a range of quality indicators covering at least church-relatedness, context-relatedness, fitness for purpose, clarity of purpose, clarity of learning outcomes in relation to purpose, alignment of activities and personnel in relation to purpose, appropriateness of assessment in relation to purpose, impact and fruitfulness in relation to purpose, holistic nature of outcomes, dependence on God, and love for God and neighbor. The challenge will be appropriate flexibility, appropriate simplicity, appropriate rigor. It may be that guidelines for local or national groups to build their own church- and context-specific QA assessment toolkits could be helpful."

RTS/IY "The learning, assessing, and recognition process must be developed with the collaboration of the church and its mission endeavors, where the identification of learning, assessment of learning, and recognition of learning in the mission of the church will be counted. *Identification of learning*: There needs to be a process for the identification of learning. Identify what the person has already learned in life and experience (identifying particular/relevant experience through comparing, contrasting, analyzing, reflecting, etc.), through learning from a mentor (providing information and helping articulate what has been learned), through shared learning (from peers or other practitioners and learners), etc. *Assessment of learning*: evaluating direct observations, self-analysis/assessment, preparation of an individual/communal learning plan, mapping or identifying personal learning needs, preparation of reports or write-ups. *Recognition of learning*: at an institutional level, (a) selection of trainers/mentors with specialized training for NFTE, (b) official certification, and (c) maintenance of a national or a regional register."

RTS/BR "NFTE groups undertake their tasks differently. Maybe some groups should set primary competencies, secondary competencies, and tertiary competencies. What we must create is an environment where NFTE can flourish by itself. NFTE encompasses different kinds: grassroots and higher-level NFTE. The grassroots [forms] speak people's language, they live and survive amid poverty, the caste system, illiteracy, and many oral cultures. Let NFTE grow by itself according to local needs. Asian learners are field-dependent, community-oriented learners; their learning cannot be toward 'independent accumulation of knowledge.' Jesus taught many things without drawing explicit conclusions; he mostly used stories that made people think. When the West says 'three points,' Eastern cultures say 'three stories.' Only local facilitators know how people's minds and thinking work. Biblical literacy, discipleship formation, missional equipping, community serving, and personal formation in spiritual and family life are a few areas of focus to consider in enhancing quality and validation processes."

RTS/HX "Attitude and purpose are key in the process of validation. NFTE initiatives need to be validated for what they contribute to the church and mission. NFTE programs are not intended to be a rigid form of education, rather an instrument of change helping the mission movement grow faster and wider. It prefers learners to continue in their local settings, creatively interacting with their church and community. Validation efforts must take this value of flexibility and learner-orientation with much study on its forms and methods. Quality checks are necessary. It should preferably be a combined effort where the church's expectations are the guiding lines toward which other training tracks help set out the validation paths and policies. If this is not the case, accrediting agencies could create a whole distinct plan for this purpose in consultation and agreement with the nonformal trainers. Another option would be to obtain membership with recognized global bodies. In any of this, we must ensure that the distinct context, distinct vernacular, distinct content, and the distinct learners are respected on their own terms, knowing that the learners' knowledge and experience in life has a vital place in the process. Liberal arts education does this very well in many places."

Summary: Respondents affirmed the need for quality assurance or validation for NFTE programs, while suggesting that it need not be complicated with unnecessary mechanics. They observed the importance of considering the diversities of NFTE programs and the unique features therein as part of their distinctive value. There was emphasis on the validation/QA process being based on the training design, procedural efficiency, and results produced. While there are multiple ways to get NFTE programs validated, the prime purpose was mentioned as service to the church and its mission in the world.

Opinions Regarding the Possibility of FTE-NFTE Collaboration

Opinions varied among the strategic leaders regarding the prospect of FTE-NFTE collaboration. Six responded "Yes," two "Maybe," and two "No."

RTS/BR "Maybe. These are the types that do things very differently in perspectival, structural, and functional aspects. Collaboration is only possible on the grounds of extraordinary humility and a sharing mentality for the sake of a common goal and common function by sharing a variety of key resources."

RTS/DT "Maybe. What we need to see is whether collaboration will remain a verbal commitment or will actualize in practice. A crucial aspect is that collaboration is not a one-time event; it is a long and humbling process to be tested by time. It involves an ongoing sharing of strengths based on genuine mutual recognition and for the growth of the body of Christ."

RTS/FV "No. FTE in South Asia is wholly governed by the Western intellectual approach, which binds FTE under constant pressure in what we call 'knowledge dissemination.' My view is that FTE will remain shortsighted about the value of NFTE. Creating a constant desire for more degrees will not grow Christianity in this area. At what point then do we envision collaboration?"

RTS/AQ "No. These are two noncompromising sectors. If collaboration involves mutuality, it is very unlikely that it will happen."

Practical Recommendations for FTE-NFTE Collaboration

RTS/JZ "To collaborate, we must think and work among real people, leaders of specific formal and nonformal organizations sitting together, eating food together, building trust, sharing vision, praying together for one another, and discovering opportunities to work together to equip the people of God for the mission of God. Then ongoing collaboration is possible. Intentionally creating friendly spaces for leaders of different institutions, both formal and nonformal, to mix and mingle, pray, and share, could be a helpful way forward."

RTS/IY "If either one claims to be a higher partner, the only one that can provide excellence in education or serve the church, true collaboration will not happen. But if the interest in TE lies in serving the church and preparing leaders contextually with ministry skills and spirituality, collaboration is possible. Three groups of people will make a reasonable resource team of academic partners to help develop criteria for NFTE: trainers/course developers and churches; mission organizations to help develop missional/ministerial expectations of learners; and contextual experts to help lay out the needs/prospects/challenges on the ground (also to serve as ongoing mentors to leaders)."

RTS/HX "Alliances for a technical resolution will not serve the purpose on their own; we must approach collaboration as an inevitability for the future of Christianity in our land. This will be possible only with selfless sharing of strengths and resources, and that is the actual challenge before us. If we are seriously considering a change, we must come away from the FTE-NFTE technicalities and think more deeply through the biblical and historical mandate given to us. Technicalities are on the periphery; we must consider the central goal of all our existence and service."

RTS/GW "Who is trying to make a profit out of collaboration is a fear at both ends. Funding and finance sharing also raise a critical issue in this. The situation takes an unhealthy momentum when driven by fears of being utilized or victimized by the other. We must change gear to see how we can get our trainees/students to serve the church in their localities. Mission is God's, and all its forms are entrusted to the church. Only if FTE and NFTE can willingly listen to each other, and agree on the needs of the church, can they walk together."

RTS/FV explained how a formal school in his country incorporated nonformal elements in its training thus: "(1) The curriculum being shaped as a thought-through response to the ground realities and needs of the local church. (2) The student body being made up of those who fulfill pastoral roles or are committed to vocational ministry on the one hand, with a larger number being made up of 'lay people' (Christians in the marketplace who provide leadership and services both to the church and to society through their professions). (3) Programs that are tailor-made to meet the broader needs of the church. (4) The 'local initiatives' creating study centers in select localities to serve the needs of rural churches for formal and nonformal training. (5) Developing education and training initiatives in response to requests from partner churches and Christian organizations. (6) Ministry-enrichment seminars that are organized in collaboration with regional pastors/fellowships for church leaders lacking formal education (seminary faculty spend a one-off full day teaching such leaders). For meaningful collaboration, (a) formal theological institutions must recognize the valuable resources of knowledge and experience they possess in their faculty and library, which are for the purpose of serving the educational and training needs of local churches. This commitment to the local church must be effectively communicated through a church-relations strategy. (b) NFTE programs often look to seminary leaders for consultancy and expert review of the programs they conduct. This could also be a point of collaboration. (c) Established seminaries could provide an NFTE program with a 'Partner' status, and thereby enhance its credibility as a program of training and promote its accountability to uphold quality standards for the benefit of its users."

RTS/EU "Collaboration in its real sense will ensure that education is not limited to or finished in a particular period of schooling but makes persons lifelong learners building the church and transforming the society. For this, FTE and NFTE should gladly agree to share their treasures for the growth and mission of the church. Tensions exist. Maybe we should think and plan unconventionally."

RTS/CS "The collaboration between FTE and NFTE is only possible when the content, importance, and influence of both are understood and taken at face value. The misunderstanding is only because we tend to accord undue importance to formal theological education and exercise an outright nonrecognition of the nonformal. The main problem is that we don't dare to address the right question, which is all about the church and not necessarily about formal or nonformal TE."

RTS/BR "Collaboration is essential for TE in this part of the globe to reduce the Western influence and university model that fail to produce the intended effect on local settings where churches are. Evangelical TE started very well, but in the mid 90s we shifted to the Western model of academia and kept up with the slogan "Publish or Perish," shaping training in a merely intellectual dimension which is not helping the formation of local Asian churches and missions. The elite shape of the seminary and the predominantly grassroots function of the flourishing church are not matching at any point."

RTS/AQ "The essential struggle is between the formal world's need for bridge-building and the nonformal's need for quality assurance. We are talking collaboration amid these pulls, and it involves many more partners, from credible academics to local men and women. Considering the needs of the churches in the nations, NFTE may need to lead upfront as the mission-hastening sector, while FTE should be supporting, and firmly undergirding."

Summary: Responses from the Regional Training Strategists recognized the strengths in both FTE and NFTE methods and affirmed the need for quality assurance or validation for training programs. They pointed out pertinent issues in South Asian TE, including its lack of clarity in goals and its Western cognitive orientation in process, and they shared in detail various dimensions of quality assurance for NFTE. The training experts made sharp observations regarding the disconnect between the two forms, while simultaneously being supportive of the concept of collaboration. Repeated mentions of the vocation of theological educators/trainers to serve the mandate of the church featured in their responses. Despite the odds, they hoped that through reaffirming the existing connections, better collaborations could be achieved in congeniality through listening, humility, relationships, and prayer.

Actualizing Collaboration on the Ground: Beyond Talks and Thoughts

This was about having churches, mission organizations, theological seminaries, nonformal ministry education initiatives, Christian nongovernmental organizations, and accrediting agencies around a table of dialogue toward collaboration. Regional Training Strategists shared their thoughts on this prospect.

RTS/GW "Our problem is a lopsided theology. We have lost our center, which is the church. This is the product of the university model of educational philosophy. We have replaced church with the seminary and ultimately lost. The church is the only authentic, organic body that can effectively do lifelong learning, discipleship, ministry formation, and mentoring. It is toward the church that we should all be moving in terms of future development. From my experience I would say that it must be the church, not the seminary, that commissions its ministers; this makes every function of TE clear and interconnected. Reclaim the church, the center. Make systems collaborate to serve the church."

RTS/CS "Seminaries must encourage their students to engage in nonformal learning activities. They must work with churches and organizations to encourage NFTE; conduct awareness programs with leaders from all these churches and organizations. My country is gullible regarding false teachings and false prophets. There is a lack of spiritual and theological maturity as people show a cynical attitude toward formal education. Most leaders are solely dependent on their years of experience in ministry, and they tend to downplay the significance of formal TE. Moreover, because of the prevailing social learning culture (emulating others), churches are splitting and breaking further away and starting new independent congregations. Similarly, a genre of Bible colleges also has mushroomed regardless of standards and quality of training and education. Some merely offer certification for social recognition rather than educating people for life and service. The discipleship training programs are not properly designed to train servant leaders with a heart of integrity and skills to handle the holistic ministry of the church. The necessity for integral mission is not identified by the church. The church exists to convert people and have church gatherings for worship, while many social concerns are either overlooked or counted as the job of parachurch organizations. The church, consequently, has lost out in making a transformative impact on the community. The Great Commission is understood merely for converting people, rather than teaching, training, and 'making disciples.' The meaning of the Great Commandment – loving God and loving your neighbor – has not been properly grasped. Ultimately the church has largely failed in becoming the 'salt and light' of the earth. Any strategy must aim at changes in this area."

RTS/IY "We need to develop a culture of lifelong learning among various stakeholders – accrediting agencies, churches, mission organizations, training institutions, educationalists, church members/leaders, professionals, and marketplace evangelists. They need to be equipped in discussions, dialogues, motivation, affirmation, resource-sharing, synergizing, assessments, recognition – all toward the mission of teaching the Word and training people in ministry."

RTS/DT "I guess that there will be different ways forward in different contexts. The current generation, young and old, prefer competency-based short courses. This fits well with their busy engagements in life and also gives them individual freedom to select according to their learning needs. Macro-credentialing is not the preferred focus for all; not everyone is crazy for the highest degrees anymore. People look for learning that brings change in their life and ministry; they want to experience this change for themselves. Of course Asians value paper degrees and recognized titles. Yet, in Asian countries, education is more than that; it is about relationships, competencies, and advanced engagement in community. Unless seminaries change to see the changing worldview of education, they will die of ignorance and irrelevance."

RTS/EU "We need to train bi-vocational pastors and leaders. Churches are not willing to provide full support to pastors as in the days gone by. Collaborative plans need to point to the growth of the church in the land."

RTS/HX "The FTE-NFTE divide is essentially a matter of priority and hierarchy in theological and ministry education. It is something that might remain because it is deep-seated in social conditioning. NFTE is foundational in the sense that it exists 'to equip all God's people' and it affirms the purpose of TE as empowering all God's people. FTE focuses on equipping equippers to teach the truth. Concerned stakeholders and resource teams should come together and commit (beyond discussing) to cutting loose from their siloed spaces. There are different levels of ministry involvement and service, but a vision of collaboration must see everyone's significance in the kingdom of God. Together we must find ways to address the superior-inferior polarities. God's kingdom is built only with every-member discipleship and participation. This is perhaps the only reason that can bring institutions around the table. Churches focus only on their routine weekly activities; unlike the formal educational schools, they do not have trained personnel, learning resources, funding mechanisms, or even a strategy to undertake this task. This is where collaboration matters."

RTS/AQ "By all means it should not be about replacing formal TE with the nonformal. FTE would lack effectiveness if students were not made lifelong learners. Conversely, NFTE would be worthless if they failed to build on educational principles and values. Creating awareness of bridge-building is necessary; and of course, a bridge should enable you to walk both ways."

RTS/JZ "When FTE and NFTE remain unwilling, maybe subtly, to recognize and approve each other, we may need to find a third focus where they can serve for the advancement of God's mission. Jesus declared his mission as the 'building of the church,' and for the church he died and for the same he will return. Having this as the central thought, we may work together."

RTS/BR "We need deep discussions, sharing of hearts, building of trust over time – before specific collaborative projects are attempted. Also, there must be a genuine mutuality, not just 'big brother' helping 'little brother.' The question should not be 'How do we do quality assurance for NFTE?' Such a question implicitly assumes that we already have effective quality assurance for FTE, but that NFTE is lagging. The real question is, 'How do we know that our leader development work is working – both in FTE and in NFTE?' To put it another way, the right approach to training evaluation should be relevant and usable for everyone, both formal and nonformal. The same foundational principles are equally applicable and should be present in both. Evaluation must focus on the design and the process, not just outcomes. Also, outcome evaluation must focus on long-term impact, not just short-term exams. Long-term evaluation will only occur properly in the community of the churches. Any approach to evaluation must nurture capacity in how to think about leader development, not just be a list of boxes to tick. If the approach to evaluation consists of a list of boxes to tick, then the participants will certainly produce the 'quality outcomes,' but will do so in ways that are often very poor quality. If there is a certificate attached to it, then people will sign up to get the certificate and some, perhaps many, will do the bare minimum just to get the certificate. If evaluation is a list of boxes to tick, then the training ministry will try to sell to people on the list, using the certificate as 'bait.' What the ministry should be doing is building the local capacity to do high leader development in the first place – not selling a list. Evaluation must be to improve the quality of the training, not to get a piece of paper or to establish someone as 'qualified.' The formal and nonformal must serve the informal. Informal is where the leader development occurs, not in the classroom. Training in the New Testament – the Gospels, Acts, and Epistles – occurred in the context of life. It was not its own detached 'thing.' It was woven throughout the life of the churches. The idea of 'standards' is from the industrial revolution, mechanical mass production. Formation was not mechanized in the New Testament – it was always individualized, in the context of deep community: organic, experiential, and transformational. The role of a 'training ministry' – whether formal or nonformal – must be to nurture the vision and capacity of the local churches to do their own holistic training work that is woven naturally into the life and ministry of their churches."

RTS/FV "Keeping all the doctrinal and theoretical differences apart, there should be one vision, and that is to win our land for Jesus. Many leaders may execute NFTE activities individually but there should be strategic initiatives in training, equipping, and building leaders for the church. A good monitoring system will lead leaders to measure the progress of the output and the outcome. This also will allow us to identify the percentage-wise growth of Christianity in geographical areas, and to assess the gaps to reinvest in or develop new strategies to reach those who have not yet heard the gospel. Collaboration plans may need to have a separate focus on the city, urban, and rural areas, to help the learning levels of participants and localized ownership of the churches. There should be surveys and studies from time to time to identify gaps and develop future programs aligning with the needs of the marketplace. This may be shared with international donors to visualize areas of investment for the church to flourish. Churches must lead the training of the believers, and if seminaries are at all involved, they must assist and help in the training and establishing of the churches. Theological education must be made available in every language possible. Resources must be made available in as many languages as possible. Local churches and networks of churches in unreached areas must be trained and well supported so that they can effectively reach their regions. Theological education and training must be made cheaper and more accessible. The church must drive the designing of curriculum and training. Seminaries, NFTE, NGOs, marketplace missions – all should share the common vision, the common ground of mission, and share resources."

Summary: TE strategists responded at great length and in depth to the questions on collaboration. The challenge and invitation they set is to move beyond discussion tables to action fields, where there is much work to do, much giving to take place, selfless recognition to be exemplified, and great perseverance for the well-being of the church of Jesus Christ to be envisioned. Bi-vocational, bridge-building, salt and light, being one body, and building the kingdom are a few expressions that indicated the theological underpinning for the collaborative frame. FTE and NFTE, and all our organizations and stakeholders in TE, are challenged to consider the agenda of the "church," warranting an attitudinal and functional shift. The strategists also emphasized the need for empathetic listening and ongoing contextual study so that local communities will move on with concrete awareness of their geographical particularities and the state of Christianity in their surroundings.

Listening Process 3: Focus Group with National Catalysts

The six participants represented young and old educators, and both experts and novices in the field of theological/ministerial training representing South Asian nations. Focus group interactions started off with the FTE-NFTE dynamics in the region. The discussions naturally took their own route to the mission to be accomplished in their countries. Participants expressed concern and urgency over the state of Christianity in their nations and the enormous burden this places on the training sectors. Highlights from the discussion are presented thematically below.

FTE Should Not Be Labeled Irrelevant

Although FTE has many irrelevant aspects in methods and contents, participants contended that FTE itself is not irrelevant. They observed it having an irreplaceable role in the sphere of education and training. This should not be ignored in discussions and strategic planning.

No One Is Perfect

Participants in the focus group maintained that flaws are not particular to any one sector; both FTE and NFTE have issues in spiritual and ministry formation, content selection, assessment, faculty/facilitator formation, character formation, and many more. Effectiveness depends largely on the vision and commitment of the local leaders who run the program. Pooling strengths in mutuality and a genuine aspiration to serve the kingdom purpose should make the agenda work. It was observed that generally, neither of the sectors seems willing to freely give away its specialized claims in the name of partnerships/networking. The common fear that emerged was that FTE's openness to associate with the nonformal or offer it some recognition might eventually make NFTE lose its identity. As grants, stakeholder interests, and denominational controls play their part, the question of profit and loss has subtly been sustaining the tension.

The Amount of Salt Needed to Give Flavor to the Nation

Participants felt that the focus should be the overall vision for Christian presence and sustainable growth in the nations. Expecting the nations in South Asia to be 100 percent Christian would be unrealistic. However, they suggested that we should navigate the training efforts to ensure an adequate amount of "salt" to give flavor to countries and subcontinents. This was shared as a pressing concern in countries like Bangladesh and Bhutan, where the Christian population is very low.

Church Believers Must Not Be Overlooked: They Are the Mission Force

The group discussed the core value of believers in the training scenario. Pastors increasingly tend to be the protectors of church property and managers of internal affairs. Unfortunately, most of them have nothing to do with leading people to Christ. One of the participants stated, "It is not the pastor who grows the community; most of the time it is the committed member who does the job." Believers need equipping and enabling to lead people to Christ and grow the community of believers in depth and strength. In the past they did it spontaneously in their communities; but now, with sociological shifts that are altering community patterns, they need to be trained and prepared for the task of mission and evangelism. By paying exclusive attention to pastors and leaders and ignoring the members, the participants felt the kingdom mission in our pluralistic neighborhoods was reduced.

"Effective Internships" to Balance Knowledge and Engagement

There were mentions of "effective internships" (i.e. not in name only) being initiated through collaborating with churches and mission organizations. The group commented that properly designed and supervised internships can open up significant opportunities for FTE-NFTE collaboration. This would bring into balance the intellectual component and practical engagement to the benefit of the multifaceted needs of the church. However, the strategies must consider diversity such as unreached ethnic groups, multicultural cities with migrant populations, and the diaspora. Participants suggested that TE in the region should assume new methodologies to be conversant with the changing world where economic, religious, and political disparities make people indifferent to matters of faith and God. People need to take Christian mission seriously and engage willingly.

Navigating the Consistent Growth of Christianity in the Region

The group affirmed that the growth momentum must be marked by many more new believers following Christ and not by biological or split-church growth. Discussing mission opportunities to enhance Christianity's continuing growth in the region, the group commented on taking advantage of the trends of migrants, diaspora, a women/family focus, bi-vocational initiatives, digital technology, and marketplace evangelism.

TE Addressing People's Basic Questions

Participants expressed that the TE enterprise must seek to provide answers to a few basic questions: Who is responsible for discipleship formation and witnessing? How could the TE tool be used to revive the local church to assume its vocation in our broken and changing world? How should I live and serve as a Christian in my country at this time? What is most crucial for my people to learn to grow in faith and mission in the current socio-religious climate? Participants suggested that instead of creating more sophistication, trainers/teachers should start with addressing basic questions like these.

Minimal Presence of the "Church" in TE Curricula

The group recommended that ways should be found to translate theological knowledge into the language and situations of ordinary people. TE is for all, and this translation of knowledge would help every member in the church be equipped daily in faith and life. Participants maintained that formal and nonformal initiatives need redefinitions in this regard. How much of this vision is reflected in the FTE/NFTE curriculum is debatable in the context. Most trainers/educators are comfortable in their cocoons and silos, managing their own affairs. The group insisted on the need for persons who will see the grand vision of Christianity and shape institutions in a paradigm change.

Jesus's Method Was Simple, Relational, and Organic

There was a distinct discussion on Jesus's model. Participants used the discussion to verbalize how the Lord Jesus, in his earthly ministry, served in the field, with people, relating and listening, as well as trusting, engaging, and assigning. His was a natural system woven around human relationships. It was organic and devoid of complexities that would scare people away. Jesus's approach competently helped people find meaning in life and purpose for action. Learners ardently sought out his teaching. In contrast, everything is highly sophisticated within theology and theological education, and institutions are straining for minimum numbers for immediate survival.

Listening Process 4: Personal Interviews with Global TE Leaders

The eight personal interviews held during this process were rich in information, expertise, and experiential reflection. This process was initiated separately to gather views from leaders in a personal conversational space. The main ideas derived from the feedback are presented below without naming the person/s.

- *FTE is vital:* A couple of interviewees insisted that the approval or validation of NFTE programs should not happen at the expense of traditional seminary education. Disregarding or neglecting FTE's significant place in training will put the health of Christianity at high risk in the long run. They pointed out the need for FTE to grow more holistic and church-ward, and also warned about disregarding it altogether. A leader said, "It is not either/or in the case of FTE and NFTE; both are indispensable to Christianity's thriving."
- *Fear of utilitarian attitude:* In many places the current widespread interest of FTE to bring on board the large number of NFTE programs is not fully welcomed, for various reasons. Interviewees mentioned that NFTE has a fear of being utilized to sustain FTE institutions, many of which are already losing out on student numbers. Many NFTE leaders assume that even with only peripheral associations with NFTE, seminaries nationally and globally are trying to handle the questions about relevance and ministry formation in an easy way. If such is their attitude, the interviewees observed that it will hamper the large-scale mission efforts by NFTE, and we will see the church decline in local settings.
- *Unrealistic number games:* There were remarks about "number games" challenging the authenticity of training impact. Massive "number games" in programs and planning require authentic attention, they stated. It was advised that the initial enrolments in a formal or nonformal program should not be confused with the actual number of outputs. Propagating bizarre assumptions, such as that one trainee will train five more, and creating enormous calculator multiplication is far from the reality on the ground, stated one interviewee. The paradigm must shift to building up

every member in the local church in his or her calling and gifting. Independent numbers unsubstantiated by active records and follow-up for scrutiny will only accelerate persecution in the nations. This is where evaluation, transparency, and accountability matter.

- *The secular world is ably tackling formal-nonformal reciprocity:* The personal interviews recognized the tremendous shifts in the world in recent decades toward "nonformal" practices. Influenced by multiple factors in the globalized world, education, religion, the arts, and business are embracing "nonformal" initiatives, as one leader commented. Interviewees spoke of the need to wisely explore how the world outside TE, at least in the educational field, looks at the situation, and to innovate strategies without elevating one over the other. One leader commented that each country will have models integrating the formal and nonformal and TE leaders might explore them appropriately in their strategies.
- *Enough talking:* Several comments were along this line. Traditional TE promoting siloed learning and detaching itself from an ecclesial focus was identified as an ongoing struggle. Interviewees reflected on much of the funding and resources being spent on the maintenance of infrastructures and global educational events. Caught up in rigid academization, people are losing the capacity for constructive listening to the church in their localities. "With a strict number of years (students must be done with studies and get out of campus by this date), bound to campus, confined to ad hoc events (that may or may not be relevant to the learner), and unchecked transferring of information, the training systems need transformation. We have done enough talking," said an interviewee. Not more talking; we need proper listening, and more flexibility to get more people into action.
- *Noninclusive training systems:* To address the needs of all God's people – the entire community of faith – seminary education obviously has limitations, remarked interviewees. They observed that the formal seminary system is inaccessible for children, teens, women, the poor, and the elderly, who all need to be equipped in their own gifts and callings. The church has access to all these groups, or it can explore access across the strata of society. Given that the law of the land is enforcing stricter policies on Christian activities in

many countries, respondents pointed out the urgency to strengthen existing church bodies to be more efficient.
- *Belling the cat:* We need knowledge and practice; we need FTE and NFTE. "Who will bell the cat? Who will have courage to do things differently?" asked a leader.
- *The church growing irresponsive or irresponsible?* Interviewees also indicated that churches seem unwilling to take up the responsibility to equip their members. According to one interviewee, this is an area worth further research. "How can we renew churches to become the seedbed as in Acts, amid the internal and external problems? To reorient churches from rigidity and routines back to mission life, we need a collective momentum. A single-focused collective momentum – what will that look like?" asked another respondent.
- *Lopsided theology that corners the church:* There were sharp comments regarding high-level discussions and alliances that fail to impact ministry on the ground. Some of the interviewees opined that new forms of accreditation or new alliances between the formal and nonformal cannot resolve the tension. One of them said, "The real issue is a lopsided theology where the church is getting isolated from the training agenda of our institutions as well as programs." Another remarked, "The gospel process is simple, we just need to follow the method of Jesus and the disciples. The greatest of human schema will only work through prayer, spiritual warfare, daily Bible study, and sincere relationships with people. Because this is simple, this is ignored too."
- *Fragmented learning putting believers at risk:* Interviewees recognized the support of the Western world for the growth of TE and mission elsewhere. "Local churches will not commit to support formal TE. Volunteerism is rarely practiced in most parts of the region. As funds and resources are necessary to make ideas work, people would rather reduce to their own little kingdoms of ministry, with their own training programs. Churches and seminaries are turning inward, to their own internal issues, which are many." Another respondent said, "Occasional events are sometimes called NFTE – in certain cases they offer certification too. Teachers come from different countries on a week or so's 'mission trip' and leave the

locals with little knowledge of something. How can we call such activities 'education'? FTE and NFTE must have proper educational designs and goals. Fragmented teachings are causing divisions and the proliferation of heresies."

- *Quality Assurance is key:* Interviewees were generally appreciative of quality assurance in training programs. But some of them warned against the discussion of QA being targeted only at NFTE, when FTE was also seen to have intrinsic quality issues. "When goals change, the educational methods change; when methods change, the patterns of assessment change; when patterns of assessment change, it calls for a total revisiting of the overall practice of training and its situated impact. Therefore, quality is a holistic concern; both formal and nonformal education encounter profound challenges in this area."
- *We are one body:* Some statements highlighted the need to come back to biblical and historical foundations. "Learn the methods in the Gospels and book of Acts. Learn from the apostle Paul. The self-orientation of our institutions must be corrected with the sending [mission] agenda as in John 20:21." Another commented, "Will seminaries, churches, and other mission institutions agree that they are called to be '*one body*'? That they are not independent entities doing their own thing, but serving the kingdom purpose by freely giving their divinely handed strengths and resources? This calls for a shift in mindset." "The actual debate is about the nature and function of the church. According to Ephesians 4:11–13, the purpose is that the body of Christ is equipped to grow into maturity. This is more than just sending students as missionaries; it is a whole-church business: everyone actively engaging in their specific places in God's mission."
- *Altruistic collaborations? Magnanimous persons-in-action on the ground?* Respondents reflected on what we really need at this point in history. "Let there be more publishing, more consultations, more partnerships, and funding. But what we really need is a clarity of purpose, selfless collaborations, and generous persons-in-service to make things work practically on local ground."

Overview of the Listening Process

The listening process in the study had four methods, and these are the key findings from each.

1. Opinionnaire 1: Listening to lead trainers and faculty from South Asia:
   - Both FTE and NFTE have profound strengths and flaws, and between them are multiple blurred areas.
   - The recognition or validation of NFTE programs is a great prospect, although it is a complex process.
   - Collaboration is desirable and good, but intrinsic issues will continue to prevail, curtailing missional impact.
   - Churches in South Asia have distinct training needs across the spectrum of discipleship, leadership, and mission.

2. Opinionnaire 2: Listening to regional TE strategists in South Asia:
   - There are deep-seated gaps prevailing between FTE and NFTE in the region.
   - There is no shortage of consultations and high-level events; yet the agendas are not effectuated in the local contexts of church life.
   - Accreditation fits the formal sector, but it will not help the nonformal; it requires a different process. Validating or ensuring quality for the nonformal is complicated but might resolve several of the existing concerns.
   - Building relationships, attentive and respectful listening, humility, a sharing mindset, dependence on God, and prayer are key to the future of Christian endeavors. Ongoing learning and research on country/strata specifics are crucial in the process.
   - Revisiting the need/goal of the church is primary; future strategies should be shaped from there.

3. Focus Group: Six national leaders/training practitioners from South Asia:
   - Most training is run independently of churches and the outcomes are not useful for the mission of the church.
   - The nonformal seems to be leading in numbers and capturing a broader attention. However, failing to sustain transformative formal

education will put the future health of Christianity in the region at risk. Balance is key.
- A larger and clearer picture of Christianity's status and challenges must drive our vision; more thinking, sensing, listening, and learning are needed.
- Any form of training collaboration must help the church recognize its commission to go and make disciples, and help it to assume the duty of preparing every member. A change in mindset is paramount in equipping all to become "salt and light" in the region.

4. Personal Interviews:
   - Clarify the *goal* of training in the region; it must be the equipping of the church to equip its people.
   - The church is the center; the church must be the agent and the chief stakeholder. Every other institution should commit to support the church to keep its footing steady in mission.
   - High-level discussions and research do not impact the believing community's quests on the ground.
   - Get people from the spectrum of training in the nation and explore where and how they could serve each other selflessly as "one body."
   - Our discussions must be geared toward belling the cat for an altruistic, practical collaboration for the well-being and growth of the church.

This process of listening spawned both curiosity and commitment regarding possible collaborations of the formal and nonformal TE for the well-being and thriving of the church. While some statements and observations in the data might sound critical or idealistic, they are invaluable in that they are real-time voices from the region. Much of the discussion on collaboration starts around the claims and complaints regarding "quality" between the formal and nonformal. The next chapter attends to certain dimensions of this matter to help with envisioning the forward trajectory of training in South Asia.

Listening Processes 2–4: Global, Regional and National Voices 97

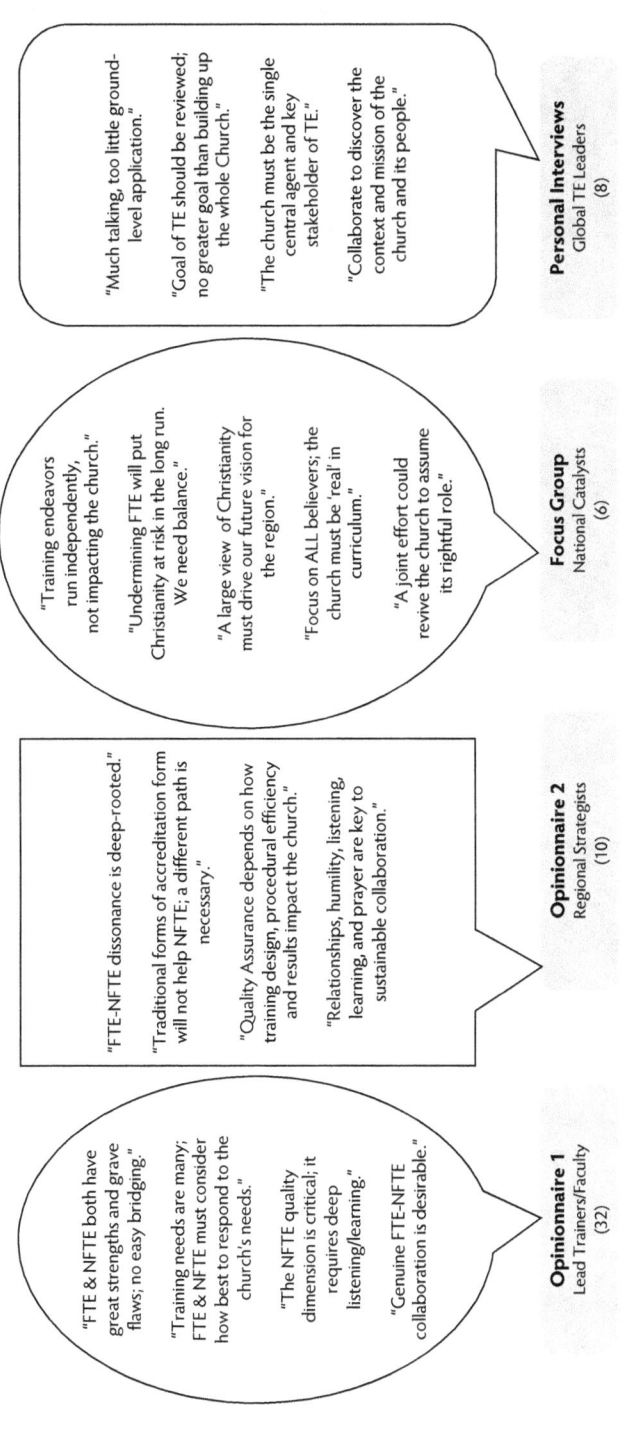

Figure 4.1 South Asia Listening Process Summary

5

Thinking Quality, Context, Collaboration, and the Church

The global-level listening process initiated by ICETE during the pandemic season entered deeper waters than had ever been envisaged. As participants, those from any sector of TE could confidently share their ideas, reflections, and opinions in the chat box during virtual events and subsequently in the forum discussions.

The ICETE online events on "Formal and Non-Formal Theological Education in Dialogue" came up with significant observations. The Thematic Analysis[1] was based on eighteen forums involving seventy-six participants from thirty-four countries across six continents. Figure 5.1 shows the analysis of responses on formal-nonformal confluency.

The following Action Points resulted from the Thematic Analysis:

- **Action Point 1:** Continue conversations between the FTE and NFTE sectors for the purpose of *identifying common goals and ways to work together.*
- **Action Point 2:** Determine ways outside accreditation to *provide a mutually satisfying standard of accountability.*

---

1. https://ecte.eu/wp-content/uploads/2022/09/FTE-and-NFTE-Thematic-Analysis.pdf Analysis summary of C-21/22 Consultation carried out by Julie Shoemaker, a ThM student at Dallas Theological Seminary and intern, under the supervision of Michael Ortiz.

- **Action Point 3:** *Gather respected NFTE leaders to create a quality standard* for the NFTE.
- **Action point 4:** FTE and NFTE to further *research and test competency-based methods of education* for effectiveness. This educational method will require a shift in mindset for those in both FTE and NFTE.
- **Action point 5:** FTE and NFTE to consider what *continuing education they can offer to facilitators.* This can be both to further education in the development of their disciplines and in teaching methods.

The findings call for more meticulous systems for quality assurance (QA) and newer expert tracks to take things further.

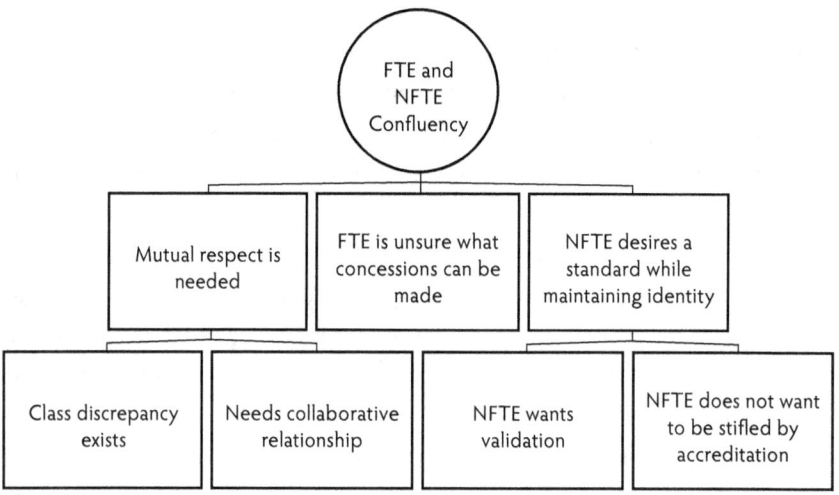

Figure 5.1 FTE-NFTE Confluency: Thematic Analysis of the ICETE Dialogue

The Question of "Quality"

The term "quality" is relative in meaning. The definition of "good quality" of a program in one context may not necessarily be correspondingly assumed in another. Quality is determined differently – on the grounds, for example, of set objectives, fixed skills indicators, points of contextual relevance, competencies acquired by the learners, and/or the broader impact on the transformation of the community at large. We speak of multiple fronts too, such as the QA of a student, course, or program of an institution, each addressing distinct goals, functions, and outcomes. From the blueprint of a program to its sustainable impact on the larger community, everything can come under the scrutiny of quality.

Single-track quality standards set by external agencies and with which educational settings should comply have inherent strengths as well as raising explicit concerns. While such procedures are essential in any educational continuum, they might tend to overlook the holistic development of learners, including learning approaches. Sometimes they fail in practically recognizing that educational design should be responsive to changing contextual realities.

Typically, QA reviews campus facilities, infrastructure development, faculty profiles, curricular design, contents, resources, objectives and outcomes, methods of assessment and improvement, and institutional sustainability. Most of these in the formal education environment do not have any correspondence in the nonformal. When it comes to nonformal QA, primary considerations are the goal, program design, delivery, resources, learner competencies, and intended impact, mostly in a less meticulous and less complex manner.

Setting a unified quality assurance base for nonformal programs is intricate, for various reasons: (1) There are too many types of nonformal education. (2) Nonformal training takes place across a wide range of levels of capacities and expectations. (3) Programs run with distinct focuses and goals using whichever resources and approaches suit the purpose. (4) Rather than collaborating according to a standardized common system of quality, many want to do training in their own spaces and freedom. Unlike traditional education that has a systematic path charted for standards and progress, most nonformal initiatives do not insist on educational prerequisites or standardized progressive pathways. Learning starts from any level of prelearning or skill sets. It can happen exclusively within the church, globally by online/extension programs, and locally on need-based/skill-oriented programs. Quality standards depend on the goals driving the program; they depend on learners' learning styles and needs. For instance, quality education in a church might generally require that every individual pastor and leader is holistically built up in life and mission and every believer in the faith community assumes a growth path intentionally created for his or her continuous learning and growth. As shown from the research data, in a nonformal setting we can think of QA according to the levels/stages of comprehension, competencies, engagements, and contributions, even dividing each element into specific levels, as one TE leader said; for example, competencies may be divided into primary, secondary, and tertiary. Defining these levels/stages and their specific indicators across the knowledge-attitude-behavior spectrum is a task to be worked out in close interaction with the contextual nuances of learning and doing. In this, we assume that quality assurance of NFTE must take on approaches that are different from the conventional ones. This, however, has to be envisioned from ongoing learning and engagement on the ground.

While nonformal education has its unique purposes and strengths, it encounters several criticisms too. Many programs start with immense fervor, but soon yield to mediocrity by failing in standards, transparency, and consistency. A common reason for this is that some designers and trainers of independently run nonformal programs have little or no roots in educational principles and are often left with little funding assistance. As a result, they eventually tend to settle for the minimum to meet the immediate purposes. Training initiatives with international training networks can dwindle to programmatic exercises with little local ownership or contextual integration. Lacking accountability and assessment limits effectiveness. The flexibility and openness that are strengths of the nonformal could also become grave weaknesses too.

The nonformal enterprise is criticized for overly liberalizing TE, operating without measures of quality or impact checks, and making education overly accessible for those with lower educational qualifications. Much of the social disapproval of the nonformal is owing to its inconsistency and lack of structure. Programs maintain low-level educational accountability and the administrators enjoy freedom to alter policies and even content as and when they want. Most nonformal programs do not connect to a higher education pathway, which is disadvantageous for keen learners. There have been situations when nonformal education has blocked persons from achieving career positions. For example, years of nonformal skills development in leadership may not qualify someone for a key leadership role if that person lacks formal credentials. Learning content and depth of nonformal programs could be limited, narrowly or monoculturally focused, not providing a wider worldview nor a classical theological core.

Formal education is also criticized for several issues in spite of its accredited status. Many nonformal leaders view the educational and accreditation processes of the formal with a certain level of disapproval because of the inadequate focus on the holistic formation of individuals. If QA is done on the grounds of the holistic formation of persons, several flaws may be identified in both FTE and NFTE.

The QA debate has been central in widening the gap between FTE and NFTE. As formal accrediting bodies cannot develop or impose one set of criteria that fits all, the plea of most NFTE representatives or leaders has been for a separate body developing a QA base. Tan recommends the creating of a global body to "bridge the gap between the formal and nonformal training institutions and [find] ways to create a seamless approach to theological education."[2]

Our longstanding TE practices carry several assumptions both checked and unchecked. For example, first, some assume that accreditation or some form of program recognition naturally endows quality on our education. Accreditation is supposed to assess quality and its procedures can to a certain level enhance the standards or procedures of institutions and programs. Nonetheless, virtually no accrediting format can claim to have the ultimate quality standard, because human learning is multilayered and there are dimensions of human formation that cannot be assessed by the tools and techniques of evaluation. Second, some think that the formulation of QA might naturally bridge the gap between the formal and nonformal and also the widening distance between the church and the seminary. In reality, the discussions of the QA of NFTE raise greater tension between the parties. As the research findings indicate, nonformal leaders will not easily adhere to a QA format crafted by a team authorized or initiated by a predominantly formal system. Bridging the gap is not something that can be achieved exclusively through high-level events or alliances; it has to evolve from ground-level interactions and grow through genuine relationships and spiritual service. Third, we tend to presume that "quality packages" can be

---

2. Jason Richard Tan, "Matrices for Understanding Pastoral Leadership and Implications for the Global Landscape of Theological Education," *Insights Journal* 5, no. 1 (Nov. 2019): 45.

developed for local leaders to use. But there are several profound concerns to be addressed in the context of the church and the condition of its members. QA packages will impact the urban and rural settings differently; they will take on different hues in areas of severe persecution, poverty, and extreme isolation.

While thinking about "quality education" and "quality assessment," one needs open eyes and a sensitive heart to the peoples of the world living in such a variety of sociopolitical conditions.

Recognition, Validation, and Accreditation of Nonformal Education

Terms such as recognition, validation, and accreditation are sometimes used interchangeably, yet they carry different meanings. "Recognition" is a broad term denoting the way an educational or training program is certified or accepted in a social context. "Accreditation" and "validation" are more technical terms referring to the specific standards and processes by which an educational program is certified. While "accreditation" is the official certification of an educational program or training model that is acceptable for use for a specific purpose, "validation" refers to the process of determining the level of degree to which an educational program or training model is acceptable to fulfill its intended purpose.

UNESCO's Institute of Lifelong Learning (UIL) considers

> Recognition, Validation and Accreditation (RVA) of non-formal and informal learning [as] one of the pillars of any lifelong learning policy. Consequently many countries have developed a national system for RVA. UIL considers it of the utmost importance to use RVA for integration of outcomes of non-formal and informal learning into national, regional and global qualifications frameworks.

UNESCO has established a "Global Observatory of Recognition, Validation and Accreditation of non-formal and informal learning" to monitor how different nations are building bridges between nonformal, informal, and formal learning.

"Integration into [UNESCO's] Qualifications Frameworks . . . will help ensure participants' access to education institutions and workplaces."[3]

These definitions carry practical implications. A leader with an accredited degree will have a higher probability of getting into higher official leadership roles in the church than someone who may be far ahead in knowledge and skills but lacks a formal degree. Churches on the one hand seek formal TE graduates to lead them, but on the other hand often show reluctance in providing financial assistance for their education. This makes seminaries heavily dependent on external resources. There are individuals for whom learning is a personal passion and they do so through NFTE without credentialing. Good theological monographs are often written by those without a formal theological qualification. There are theology students benefiting immensely from those outside conventional theological academia. While such contributions can be socially recognized to an extent, their contributions are heavily constrained for being outside the academic community. Discussions are underway on charting processes of validation to enable a learner to find an entry point into academia where the individual's portfolios are counted for further educational enablement.

What is validation? It is the process of assessing and recognizing a wide range of knowledge, behaviors, and competencies which a person has developed nonformally. Why validation? It advances (beyond common social recognition) learners' confidence in being an authentic part of the learning community and creates in them motivation for lifelong learning. It promotes transparency, responsibility, accountability, quality, and collaboration. Validation has essential social and personal value. It raises awareness of the intrinsic worth and rewards of learning. Theological academia in most cases will not count nonformal learning experiences as compatible with the formal, even when secular education is mainstreaming most of its applied and distant programs. Formal academia tends to analyze things from the teachers' point of view, not on the basis of the learners' experiences and skills. What should be validated is the integral nature of teaching and learning and how it impacts the learner

---

3. UNESCO Institute for Lifelong Learning, "The Global Observatory of Recognition, Validation and Accreditation of Non-formal and Informal Learning," accessed 29 September 2022, https://uil.unesco.org/lifelong-learning/recognition-validation-accreditation.

and, therefore, the church and the society. One way of doing this is to get beyond numerical grades to value the skills and competencies acquired and the ongoing ministry contributions rendered.

A key question in the recent dialogues has been, "Who sets the criteria for quality assurance to validate the nonformal training?" As discussions and debates continue, accrediting agencies, out of respect for nonformal educational initiatives, tend to let the nonformal carry on the task, and the NFTE leaders call for a separate set of principles to guide any form of validation, potentially led by those who have served for several decades in the nonformal. While the majority of learners in NFTE initiatives aspire for their programs to be formally accredited, lead trainers express their hesitation as to how this could affect the goals and outcomes of their training. For them, the distinct goals, functions, and procedures of NFTE require a distinct path of quality assurance. The formal accrediting bodies are often criticized for rigidity and closedness, where things revolve around structures and systems and not so much on the learners and their contexts. It is often commented that traditional theological academia looks down on NFTE as less valued and as an adjacent learning form.

A general recommendation is that the setting of quality standards (many prefer "quality stages" or "competency stages") for the nonformal should be done on a different track, with distinct criteria that match its values and goals. Diversity within the nonformal approaches, the numerous purposes they aim to serve, and the unique contexts they operate in, make unified quality criteria standards a distant possibility. It is observed that one cannot determine quality by an exclusive assessment of "functions"; the critically important factor is what "forms" are being served by these "functions," and whether they are doing their part well in that.

SEAN (see chapter 2) and TEE initiatives[4] offer a conceptual quality framework for their distinctive type of nonformal education. The enormous amount of learning, reflective practice, and improvement strategies that have gone into the frameworks globally cannot be underestimated. Although they grew into bigger statistics, efforts were put into practice and proven on the ground, going deeper than a mere coordination of numbers. While realizing

---

4. Hanna-Ruth van Wingerden, Tim Green, and Graham Aylett, eds., *TEE in Asia: Empowering Churches, Equipping Disciples*, ICETE (Carlisle: Langham Global Library, 2021).

that it is possible for quality claims to fail in a large-scale spread of nonformal learning, still we recognize the efforts that have gone into quality assurance at various levels, for example in design, delivery, evaluation, and modification. Training initiatives such as LeaderSource implement workable and advanced models and frameworks for quality assurance in nonformal education. The ConneXions Model[5] introduces a quality framework that runs through a program's design, process, and goal, and is portrayed through stages such as the "map," the "journey," and the "destination." Quality assurance is not a technical task at the end; rather, it is an ongoing practice before, during, and after the implementation of a program. Quality is conceived as something that runs through the entire design process, delivery, and impact check. Apart from the many ongoing efforts of quality assurance within the spectrum of nonformal TE, the secular educational world outside has tremendous resources and experiences to share, for those who do not want to reinvent the wheel.

The LDC (Chiang Mai) and GProCommission (Bangkok) led significant events on the formal-nonformal dialogues, both leaving tangible footprints. Re-Forma and TOPIC took their own initiatives to lay out quality evaluation models for nonformal field-ministry education, Re-Forma focusing on quality enhancement through "Outcome Assessment Criteria," and TOPIC being a catalyst for quality assurance for nonformal pastoral training. A recent development is that the Galilean Movement aims at strategic research on nonformal education's consolidation in terms of quality and expansion.[6]

Clearly spelled out competencies provide clear paths forward for quality assurance. However, there are dimensions where formation and transformation cannot be assessed.

Reviewing Paradigms of Learning Recognition toward FTE-NFTE Collaboration

It is apparent that there is no functional pathway for NFTE's accreditation by the traditional criteria of evaluation. This we may call a "dissonant paradigm," as shown in figure 5.2. NFTE wants to maintain its distinct identity and does

---

5. Malcolm Webber, *Healthy Evaluation Course Manual* (Elkhart: Strategic, 2010), 38–39. https://www.leadersource.org/about/models.php. Accessed 16 June 2023.
6. https://galileanmovement.org.

not want FTE formulating its accreditation criteria, for fear of being repressed or losing its distinctiveness. However, we recognize that not all forms of NFTE are the same. There are grassroots forms of NFTE and graduate forms of NFTE, the former providing education for those who are deprived of an opportunity and the latter, for those who are taking NFTE alongside their formal education at any level. Certain NFTE programs have stricter educational systems including evaluation, grading, and certification, while others simply promote learning at the individual's pace and motivation. It is also worth mentioning that many FTE institutions already have nonformal programs incorporated in their systems, and this shows the blurred areas between the two sectors. There are those among grassroots NFTE who seek some form of accreditation, while for graduates doing NFTE, this is neither a need nor always an aspiration. Normally, for NFTE to get programs accredited, they need to climb up the ladder of an equivalency process through an accredited institution, as is depicted in the "ladder paradigm" in figure 5.2.

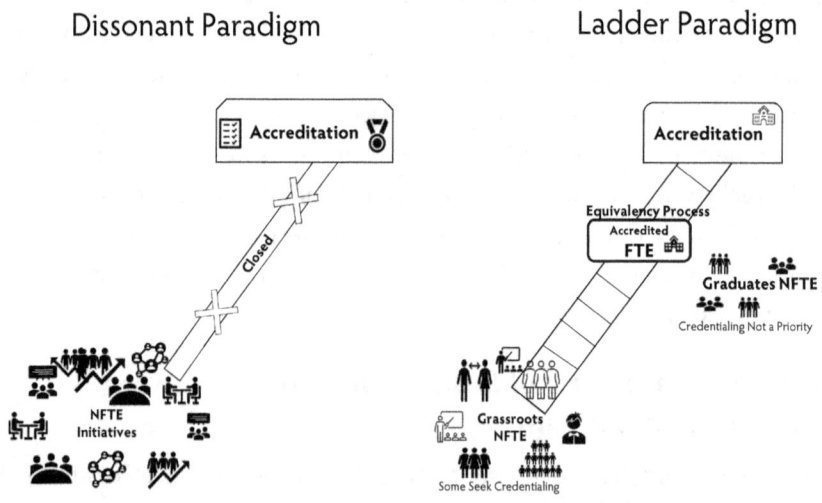

Figure 5.2 NFTE Accreditation Paradigms

The ladder paradigm is pertinent to nonformal programs that seek accreditation from a formal accrediting agency. Equivalency schemes, integrated educational pathways, and shared assessments are generally recommended to resolve concerns around quality assurance in NFTE.

However, NFTE leaders generally tend to disapprove of the idea of having their programs accredited by the evaluation criteria of formal TE or a process of equivalency, due to the distinctions in purpose and approach. For collaboration between the two, they would prefer to opt for a validation process using criteria distinctly created to evaluate the unique contextual purposes and methods of NFTE. To set out the validation criteria, a team of experts representing both streams, or those representing NFTE preferably with exposure to both streams of education, is necessary. This team will create criteria or pathways for validation considering the multiple approaches and patterns of NFTE and the existing practices of recognition of nonformal training. Still, many questions remain. Who will the team be comprised of? Who will put the team together to reach common ground, given such diversities? What is the guiding agenda to work on? Which validation pathways will ensure that multiple levels and types are included? How can equivalency tracks and connectors with the accrediting bodies be created? Should a track open to accreditation be kept at all? How will these guiding principles be established? In countries where government recognition is necessary for professional education, how much of an impact will this have? And at the end of the day, will NFTE turn into an educational stream that is more inaccessible and complicated?

Even if the accreditation prospects appear infeasible, we cannot let that affect the continuity of training or mission. Thus, if practical collaboration of FTE and NFTE is to be achieved beyond the concerns around accreditation, a symbiotic paradigm might be an option, in which "Validated NFTE" and "Accredited FTE" networks function in complementarity. As figure 5.3 represents, this paradigm is mutually synergizing and operates within the network of churches, mission organizations, marketplace endeavors, NGOs, and others. The driving factor behind this paradigm is to get both sectors to support the missional momentum so that it may continue in regions where Christianity is growing at unprecedented speeds.

The pertinent question is whether this symbiotic paradigm of equal worth and genuine mutuality is imaginable and acceptable in the context. If either one or both of FTE and NFTE choose to stick to what Ortiz articulates as the competitive wills and desires to keep the FTE-NFTE segments,[7] we will need to consider "What next?" Moreover, contrary to the voices of the research participants regarding the goal of "equipping the church to equip every member," this paradigm retains the prevalent pattern of pushing the church to the fringes alongside other organizations and keeping formal and nonformal trainings at the center.

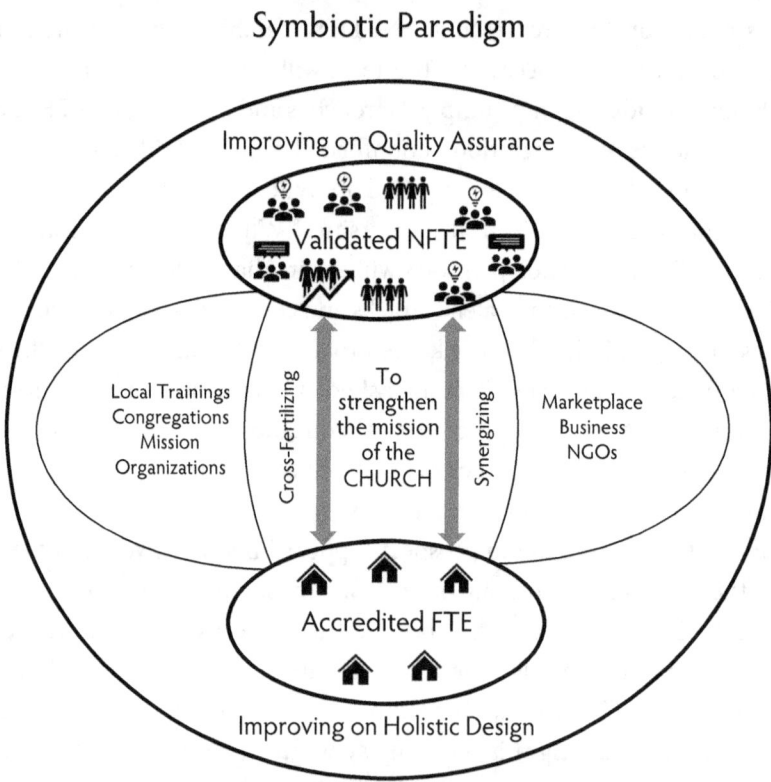

Figure 5.3 FTE-NFTE Collaborative Symbiotic Paradigm

A major issue arising from the formal-nonformal collaboration is the quality of NFTE, as the high quality of FTE is assumed based simply on its "accreditation status." Yet this premise is being challenged by many. Just because

---

7. In an informal discussion with the author.

FTE has accreditation, can all formal programs be labeled "quality education"? Does "accreditation" endow or guarantee quality? Who will judge the quality of learning, and what is the best way to do so? The formal's "big brother" attitude and the nonformal's "we're right, you're wrong" attitude block collaboration on multiple fronts. How far "quality assurance" would serve as a resolution to the need for collaboration is a persistent concern. The easiest way for many formal schools has been to incorporate informal practices into the existing formal systems, which provides better control than collaborating practically with other nonformal entities. Thus, most campuses already have distance, online, evening, or part-time courses for this purpose. Talking and writing sounds rather straightforward, while the practical collaboration of the formal and nonformal seems a distant and difficult prospect in most contexts of training. In Bolsinger's terms, "when our old map fails us, something within us dies. Replacing our paradigms is both deeply painful and absolutely critical."[8] When the gap between function and need is too big or irreconcilable, answers must be sought outside the box.

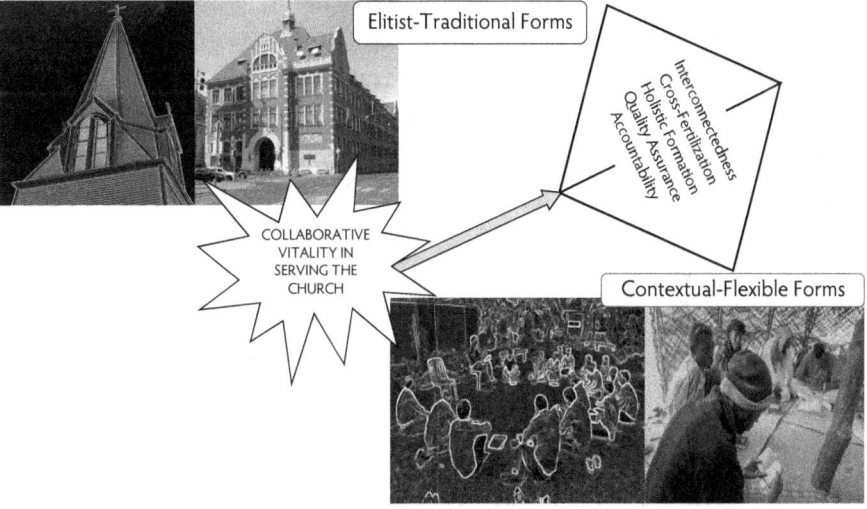

Figure 5.4 Collaborative Vitality of Traditional and Contextual Forms

---

8. Tod Bolsinger, *Canoeing the Mountains: Christian Leadership in Uncharted Territory* (Downers Grove: InterVarsity Press 2015), 93.

Valuing the Training Needs of the Church in Context

It was overwhelming to hear the research participants articulate their concerns over the gaps in TE that put the church at risk, and the urgency for formal and nonformal agencies to offer their services to churches in their localities. For churches to flourish amid the challenges in South Asia, there are several practical considerations. We maintain that church life and church growth are not mechanically forced, but organically enriched. It is a God-initiated and Spirit-led mission, in which humans have the privilege to partner. "On this rock I will build my church, and the gates of Hades will not overcome it," declared Jesus in Matthew 16:18. Therefore, the agenda is not human. This fundamental rule must guide all strategy-making and alliance-building. Providing one-size-fits-all preset compendiums might not produce the right type of fruit in diverse contexts. While foundational teachings transcend cultures and nations, the way they are taught must still make sense to people on the ground. Digging into this a little further, a few areas of consideration are given below.

The Local Church Needs Contextual Grounding

Many ecclesial contexts in the world are not "traditional." They do not have a Christian legacy or any kind of theological framework of knowing God or the Bible. In South Asian localities of first-generation Christians many might seek to "learn God's word" but with little hope of gaining a "theological degree." They do not even realize that degrees are being offered for learning the Bible. Their faith is based on experiencing Christ in the hardest of life circumstances, and not by rationally reading theology. Having them integrated straight into an FTE setting where the vast majority represents traditional Christianity can be counterproductive simply because the learners' needs and challenges are different. People do not learn things the same way, and today's educational world upholds the importance of learning varieties and learners' preferences. An interviewee from Nepal said,

> One of the states in our country values education as the "exposure of life skills." For them, people must be enabled to live and thrive in their own way. In another state, education is something that makes all people doctors or engineers. There, families and teachers push their children too hard to the extent of making them even

mentally ill. My parents trained me to see life not as a collection of big achievements, but as a meaningful process of small experiences with God as I live quietly among my people.

We in the field of theological education also hold on to distinct emphases like this. Dichotomizing knowledge acquisition and practical engagement is rarely the pattern of life in community-based cultures. The stand-alone scholastic approach in TE raises massive threats to Christianity in such contexts where along with the roots, the branches need to flourish in short periods of time. People in the church need to be equipped for those rare windows of freedom that open up for the proclamation of the gospel. These are places that *need* to "define" education in their own sociocultural terms, along with or even beyond the standardized patterns. The church in South Asia, tossed back and forth by the sociocultural and religious waves, may need to seek its own solutions to its problems to sustain its mission and to flourish. This could be the reason why the research gathered a long list of learning needs; maybe the current modes of education are failing to make learning relevant for them.

The Church Does Best through Context-Based Education

Each learning community has distinct needs in education. Imagine teaching theology, Christian ethics, or pastoral counseling using the traditional model with classic textual resources among a community of new converts who practice prostitution, steal, or brew alcohol as their only trade to make a livelihood. This might sound strange, but it is the reality of the world we are in. Their formation in faith, their goals in education, and their preferred learning styles all nullify the ready-made packages our systems have developed somewhere at certain points in history. Their skills are not in analysis and reasoning. These learners cannot be blindly integrated with a group of learners who represent the affluent, proficient, digitally competent, postmodern strata of society. Yet, when a new believer in an interior village asks for a Bible study program, we hurriedly lead him or her to a traditional FTE/NFTE setting, scarcely ever concerned about how suitable the campus culture or the program requirements might be for the prospective learner.

There are unique contextual needs to which TE must be responsive. Consider the example of prospective learners in Nepal, which used to be known as the only Hindu nation in the world until it was declared secular in 2007. In contexts where religious fundamentalism and bureaucracy prevail strongly, secularism implies something positive. The country's being declared secular was celebrated by the few Christians, who wanted to maximize their mission and presence before any further setbacks hit. Gathering energy from the toils of early missionaries who planted the seeds of the gospel amid unparalleled suffering, suddenly the efforts in evangelism and church planting flourished with this new window of freedom. Young men and women went out of the country in search of seminaries or libraries to study God's word and to serve in their homeland. Rapid "rabbit church growth" has been happening, new physical church plants have been erected, and several Bible colleges established. Yet the theological grounding and leader-development competencies seemed to be confined to shallow measures. The Christian community seemed to be failing in their focus of discipling their generation and new converts. Persecution, divisions in the church, syncretism, and heresies are on the increase, and the question is what sort of support and collaboration are needed for the future of Christianity in such nations. To serve the training needs, what should leaders or theological educators do differently with insight to balance breadth with depth and direction?

Vernacular Efficiency Speeds Up, Broadens, and Deepens Learning

An undergraduate from a seminary in India remarked:

> My struggle learning English was immense at the seminary. The sad thing is that I worked on my English language dream for all three years, but in vain. Those years would have been sufficient for me to reach my village for Christ. I still wonder why a local evangelist should get into a multi-year plan of learning in another language, spending so much money, and at the end of the day, feel so poorly trained for the work.

Non-Western ways of communication and learning are predominantly in the form of narratives, stories, poems, and rich descriptions of lived realities as people experience them. Non-Westerners make and shape theology this way too, rather than in abstract theories. The globalization of theological education has been advantageous for English-speaking, technologically affluent communities, yet it has further pushed the poor and digitally illiterate to the margins. This is where emerging churches find themselves being consigned to "nowhere." Mission among the unreached in the Majority World needs preparation in the vernacular. For a learner to be equipped well, the learning process must be in a language that is comprehensible, the learning must be concurrently practiced in the learner's own real community, the content must relate to the need areas of the learner, and the resources must be appropriate to the learner. This is in no way to denigrate English education or technical development, but rather is an invitation to think missionally of where the church must keep growing in quality and quantity.

In South Asia, people make sense of God, theology, and spirituality from their daily lives. Work and worship are not dichotomized. Theological education must be founded on the Bible, God's word, and be done through the church's congregational life, conversations in community, families' lived realities, and real-time service to one another. When people are equipped in and by their churches, their contextual realities and learning preferences or styles are taken at face value. It is here that educational practices delve deep into a strategic blending of formal, informal, and nonformal designs. The goal is to transform lives and move people to actions that they willingly and committedly take ownership of. The grand biblical story, community stories, narratives, observations, and making sense of God's plan for the world are a different way of learning, perhaps inviting us to break the "helicopter hermeneutic" that one can only gaze at from afar, in order to actualize a "bullock-cart paradigm" that one can realize and touch on the ground. Yu wrote about theological education that empowers the church, emphasizing the power of informal and blended ecclesial learning in which "the notion of integrating teaching, nurturing and socializing in church as an analogical response for integrating formal, informal and situated learning, is advocated."[9]

---

9. Carver Yu, "Engaging the Ecclesial Dimension: Theological Education That Empowers the Church," in *The Pastor and Theological Education: Essays in Memory of Rev. Derek Tan*, eds. Siga Arles, Lily Lim, Tan-Chow Mayling, and Brian Wintle (Singapore: Trinity Christian Center & ATA Bangalore, 2007), 180–81.

Flexibility and Accessibility as Natural Traits of Church-Focused TE

There are many things to do and maybe even more to undo when we start putting "church" at the center of TE discussions. As revealed in the research, traits such as flexibility and accessibility characterize context-oriented, church-ward/church-centered TE. No other institution can afford these values as naturally as the church. We see a marked lack of passion for a three-year full-time residential program in the confinement of a seminary campus. Age gaps and associated distinctions between learners also seem to be factors that make long-term programs less attractive. All types of learning, systematic or ad hoc, fit well with the church's education of students, professionals, missionaries, and every other member category. People prefer to move on with life's responsibilities and get a holistically built-in life.

Changing paradigms in the Asian context also warrant us to consider the financial sustainability of learners who have few resources for formal education. What could be a viable framework that might help each context develop and deliver its own relevant form of ongoing learning? Training in God's word and preparation for God's mission should be made possible for all, including those who have no means to pay for it. National and global TE leaders need to take this into account as new circles of alliances take shape and new grants are given away. One of the respondents, a lead trainer in Bangladesh said,

> No funds, no training. Training stops when funds stop. When the local leaders change the training patterns or materials assigned by their ministry partners or sponsors, the relational climate changes. Agenda has nothing to do with local leaders, it is mostly fixed and imposed; on the other side, local leaders cannot continue without funds. This must change, I don't know how.

Though not exhaustively, we have discussed a few ideas to help shape our thinking around training and collaboration. Highlighted is the need for contextual sensitivity, creativity, and responsiveness, so that the life and mission of the church will thrive locally and beyond from there. Much of this resonates with adult education principles, which provide a tremendous resource toward quality assurance in contextual learning designs. Nonetheless, above all procedural aspects stands the need to follow the biblical pattern of doing theology in and for the church.

Shifting the Center of TE from the University Model to the Church Model

Even before the COVID-19 pandemic, seminaries were already facing different levels of jeopardy. Mergings and closures are no longer news. On the other side, churches also are struggling to survive. As a research participant in this study wondered during the interview, "Is it that our heavy intellectual formation is making us so incapable of seeing in black and white the world's realities and the mission of the church?"

Against the persistent crises in TE and reservations about a university-centric or cloistered approach, four theologians, including Rowan Williams, the former Archbishop of Canterbury, expressed their optimism for the enterprise based on their deep-seated conviction that "theological education is an essential work of the church."[10] None of them felt that the fate of TE needed to be determined by its place in higher education. The entire conversation reminds us of the need to be attentive and responsive to the changing landscape of the world and the church. González's metaphor of a pipeline seems particularly relevant in this discussion. Wayman quotes him suggesting that the TE pipelines should be replaced by a thriving irrigation hose. As Wayman paraphrases, "In a pipeline, success is measured by how much water gets to the end: how many students go to graduate school or seminary, complete their degree, and go into ministry. But with a drip hose, 'the dripping of water is purposeful.'"[11] The water at the first hole is just as important as the water at the last hole. This is because "the purpose of theological education is mission. The purpose of theological education is to irrigate the land around it – it's not to push people forward."[12] The clarion call that must guide our thinking as trainers and educators is how to get each believer to irrigate the land wherever she or he happens to be.

Significant efforts have already been taken in this direction. Alpha[13] and BILD International[14] run programs to train the church in discipleship

---

10. Benjamin D. Wayman, "Imagining the Future of Theological Education," conversations with Rowan Williams, Justo González, Emilie Townes, and Sam Wells, *The Christian Century*, 10 February 2021, https://www.christiancentury.org/article/features/imagining-future-theological-education.

11. Wayman, paraphrasing Justo González, in "Imagining the Future of Theological Education."

12. González, quoted by Wayman. See also Justo L. González, "There's No Theological Education Pipeline Anymore," *The Christian Century*, 30 December 2020, https://www.christiancentury.org/article/how-my-mind-has-changed/there-s-no-theological-education-pipeline-anymore.

13. Alpha USA, https://alphausa.org.

14. BILD International, https://bild.org.

and leadership around the world. The training strategy of the United World Mission[15] enhances collaboration across the TE spectrum for leader-equipping in the church. Increase Association[16] models a church-based and contextually built training movement. LeaderSource[17] focuses on contextual healthy leader development using its distinct and tested model called ConneXions. ReForma[18] serves outcome-based biblical ministry training focusing primarily on pastoral formation. And GProCommission[19] focuses on the training of pastoral trainers. There are several more initiatives, including hundreds of online programs across the globe serving with the explicit or espoused goal of building the church in discipleship and leadership. Yet there is much still to be done to strengthen the locations where the church is isolated, persecuted, and uncared for, with no scope for future leadership.

Challenging the assumption that theological education takes place at academic institutions or seminaries and divinity schools, Bonfiglio remarked,

> The first seminary was not founded until 1563, when it was commissioned by the Council of Trent to serve as a *seminarium*, or "seed bed," for clerical training in the Catholic Church. Before the 16th century, theological education was already happening in and through local churches. This was true in the pre-Constantinian period, when churches offered a rigorous, three-year education process called the catechumenate which all converts had to go through before being baptized.... The invention of seminaries led the church to outsource what it had long taken to be an in-house responsibility: in-depth teaching on the Bible, theology, and the Christian tradition.[20]

---

15. United World Mission, https://uwm.org, https://uwm.org/overseas/discover/rth/.
16. Increase Association, https://www.increaseassociation.org.
17. LeaderSource SGA (Strategic Global Assistance), https://www.leadersource.org.
18. Re-Forma, "Outcomes," https://www.re-forma.global/outcomes.
19. Global Proclamation Commission for Trainers of Pastors, https://gprocommission.org.
20. Ryan P. Bonfiglio, "It's Time to Rethink Our Assumptions about Where Theological Education Happens," *The Christian Century*, 13 February 2019, https://www.christiancentury.org/article/opinion/it-s-time-rethink-our-assumptions-about-where-theological-education-happens.

In an interview session a leader from Sri Lanka said,

> As a theology professor and administrator in South Asia, what troubles me is how both formal and nonformal leaders rigidly (of course, proudly) hold on to their own DNA of training, so often forgetting [that] what they must conserve is the DNA of the church. People in the church are tired of having irrelevant theology graduates and irresponsible pastors; many want to leave the church. Full-time pastors with no continuing learning lack vision as they are ignorant of (or many of them do not want to know) the happenings in the world. Theology professors and graduates act like they are trained for some other world. They aren't good fits either in the church or in a spiritually dying world. When these (supposed) leaders fail to connect with the community with wisdom and kindness, we lose our children and youth in large numbers. Maybe the church must open its eyes to see the relevance of a bi-vocational focus in pastoral ministry and community service where we learn at least some way to connect with people out there.[21]

The call for seminaries to collaborate with churches has long been heard; often, however, this has been a not-so-welcome plea. White wrote an overview of the struggles and endings of seminaries in the US. He mentioned reasons such as declining enrolments, falling birth rates, tensions, divisions within evangelicalism, losing the trust of churches, increased secularization, and polarizing arguments on moral issues. For seminaries to survive in recapturing the interest of learners and the trust of sending churches, he makes several suggestions, including the following:

- Go all-in on hybrid models of education, offering both in-person and online courses and degrees. See this as the new normal.
- Actively seek out pastors and listen to what they feel a seminary education needs to hold for people they might send their way. In other words, listen to the customer.

---

21. Personal interview with a regional strategist from Sri Lanka, 23 September 2022.

- Embrace the contemporary Church instead of being threatened by it. Rather than seminaries seen as places diametrically opposed to any and all new wineskins, let the seminary be in the vanguard of cutting-edge thought related to the practice of ministry in a post-Christian world.
- Work collaboratively with churches to provide a seminary education, which means letting the Church truly contribute to that education in ways only the Church can. Seminaries need to work with churches to bring seminary education into the local church.
- Help faculty and staff realize that they do not primarily serve the academy but the local church, and pray for appropriate passion among the faculty to that end.
- Ruthlessly evaluate curriculum in light of what it is most trying to do, which is preparing men and women for vocational ministry. Yes, teach about the Council of Nicaea, but also teach about leading a council at church.
- Lose theological agendas, but rather teach diverging viewpoints within historic orthodoxy with fairness, building faculties with robust diversity within the framework of evangelical thought.[22]

We recognize that the missional task ahead in our world cannot be accomplished by any single institution or initiative; we need to collaborate. But what would it take for us to collaborate beyond dialogues and writings?

Understanding "Collaboration"

Institutions and organizations follow various methods to associate with others. Words are used interchangeably to express such an association – for example, networking, cooperation, partnership, and alliance. These words carry distinct meanings, but we consider the term "collaboration" in our discussion. This term best fits the purpose of team efforts in the South Asian context.

---

22. James Emery White, "The Ending of Seminaries as We've Known Them," Crosswalk, 6 June 2022, https://www.crosswalk.com/blogs/dr-james-emery-white/the-ending-of-seminaries-as-weve-known-them.html.

- *Networking* is the intentional making of human connections and relations with the specific aim of achieving a shared goal. Collaboration is the practical outworking of such networks where people join together to achieve a goal. Networking is essential in collaboration, but collaboration is more than networking.
- *Cooperation* is providing assistance or support to help others achieve their goal or receiving assistance or support from others to achieve your own goal/s. It is mostly a choice to be made, not necessarily a commitment to work together to achieve a common goal. Cooperation is essential for successful collaboration, while collaboration goes further to network to enable others to create or achieve a common goal.
- A *partnership* is where people or institutions come together through an expressed or implied commitment to pool their resources to create or achieve a shared goal. This demands more than networking, cooperation, and collaboration. Partnership assumes a deeper comingling of resources and a separate structure for the relational process. Collaboration is where people of a diverse array of entities come together, not necessarily bound contractually, but in a more open and inclusive process to create or achieve particular goals, or to resolve certain issues that concern all.
- An *alliance* is a special kind of networking comprised of multiple collaborations over a sustained period. It is even more formal and strategic than a partnership as it involves contracts and the strategically important interests of the groups involved. The term carries more weight in its larger and more strategic collaboration and its process management.
- *Collaboration* is a moderate and feasible network which is practical, inclusive, accessible, tailored to the local needs, and transparent. It is less binding than partnerships and alliances. Collaborating parties can operate independently and have complete control over the individual resources they bring to the table. It is less contractually structured. When people share deeply a goal or idea, collaborations can naturally take shape without even an institutional or organizational system. Collaboration is not a time-bound or task-

bound event; it is rather a process, open to any means to make it work. It may or may not give success, so there is less pressure on the parties involved. It may grow in time into strong alliances or partnerships, based on the direction in which relationships mature. Building trust and reciprocity is vital; it is a long and somewhat complex process to evaluate.

Collaboration can be envisioned or implemented in a variety of forms and at different levels. Types or systems of education can collaborate. Some collaboration plans remain at dialogue stage, while others reach the stage of diagrammatic depictions; a few realize collaboration in practice, because it is demanding, humbling, and confusing on all fronts.

This study has pointed to the need for "authentic or genuine collaboration," where one form of TE is not above the other and one is not taking advantage of or given a higher profile than the other. The study shows that the siloes are not just in the academic disciplines, but are even more prevalent in the thought patterns with which we lead our institutions and initiatives. Perhaps because of this, time and again respondents commented that a legitimate collaboration might be unlikely for FTE and NFTE (and the mission organizations and NGOs) in their local settings. Nonetheless, amid human institutions that keep shifting in their goals and commitments, the church and its mission need to be guarded, guided, and accomplished. Thus, a reimagining and reassuring of the center of our educational endeavors becomes inevitable. To this nucleus all else serves. For Christianity to continue thriving in South Asian soil, the landscape of the current training forms might need to change.

Genuine collaboration is practical, and Spirit-enabled. Unity of purpose, humility, congeniality, and selflessness define it. Its leadership, function, and direction exemplify the life-giving commitment that Jesus modelled. The leadership model shifts from unicentric to polycentric approaches. Handley's recent work has much to convey to the Asian mission and training endeavors in this regard. He calls for a multidirectional, polycentric vision where the essential characteristics of collaborative leadership are exemplified in line with their roots in the Bible.[23] This might sound fluid and scary to leaders as it

---

23. Joseph W. Handley Jr., *Polycentric Mission Leadership: Toward a New Theoretical Model for Global Leadership* (Oxford: Regnum, 2022).

requires risk-taking and courage to practice. The Lausanne Movement[24] and Asian Access[25] are taking intentional efforts in encouraging local leadership and decision-making as best fitting the local needs and situations. The same is true of Butler's use of an "open architecture" in collaboration, which all who commit to the compelling, high-value vision are welcome to be part of. This is a great idea for the accomplishment of the missional dream "from everywhere to everywhere," yet it is still not an easy practical task. Butler differentiates between "maintenance collaboration and breakthrough collaboration."[26] Not all collaboration is the same in purpose, nature, or outcome. Collaboration within the congregation also has become a theme of study in recent decades. When high-level leadership collaboration takes place, many overlook the essential collaborative breakthroughs needed on the ground, with the members of the church. This collaborative approach is examined by Pickard in his book *Theological Foundations for Collaborative Ministry*. "The discovery that Christians are members 'one of another' creates energy and joy in ministry and empowers the Church in an age of mission." Pickard affirms that church members and leaders will benefit from studying what has been termed mutual ministry, collaborative ministry, every-member ministry, and total ministry.[27]

Not seeing ourselves and our institutions as mechanical, independent systems but rather as part of an ecosystem of missional collaboration is necessary "in today's Great Commission context," says Cardenas.[28] An ecosystem is a "system, or group of interconnected elements, that interact as a community of organisms within its environment."[29] God's design of life and mission is well portrayed by this metaphor, where individuals and parts collaborate with each

---

24. https://lausanne.org.
25. https://www.asianaccess.org.
26. Phill Butler, "Characteristics of High Performance Ministry Networks," Synergy Commons, 2 January 2014, accessed 30 September 2022, https://synergycommons.net/resources/characteristics-of-high-performance-ministry-networks/.
27. Stephen Pickard, *Theological Foundations for Collaborative Ministry* (London: Routledge, 2009). Quotation from the blurb.
28. David Cardenas, "Viewing Missional Collaboration as an Ecosystem," *Mission Frontiers*, 1 May 2020, accessed 30 September 2022, https://www.missionfrontiers.org/issue/article/viewing-missional-collaboration-as-an-ecosystem.
29. Cardenas, "Missional Collaboration," citing "Ecosystem," Dictionary.com, accessed 20 February 2019, https://www.dictionary.com/browse/ecosystem.

other in maintaining and promoting life, based on the insights given by their own environment. In the current discussion on FTE-NFTE collaboration, as we are challenged to recenter to the church and its mission, the practical insights into the collaborative ecosystem seem of particular relevance.

> Understanding our missions environment (whether network, movement or other) from an ecosystem approach and behaving accordingly, can bring new relational and collaborative dimensions that enhance Great Commission efforts. This can also help us make greater use of collective wisdom and solve pending challenges. Organizations desiring to model ecosystem principles should consider the following:
> - Developing awareness that missions and church life is organic and not merely transactional or business. We are part of a whole, and it is not just your organization.
> - Overcoming the philosophy of utilitarianism that has done so much damage. Interactions between organizations must be born and maintained within the Great Commandment of love of neighbor.
> - Identifying the behaviors that build an ecosystem culture and commit to acting on those – collaboration, information flow, and resource sharing.
> - Mapping ecosystems to discern the environment; to know the diversity of the parties and their functions, relationships, and missions processes; to study how they behave and interrelate; and to discover what is missing.
> - Dealing with unhealthy interactions, such as organizational ego, individualism, indifference, competitiveness and predation.
> - Adapting for change and community learning. Experiences and knowledge must be combined to respond well and innovate.
> - Reflecting on the implications of an ecosystem where there are relationships with organisms with important influence on decisions, economic power, and varied cultural background.[30]

---

30. Cardenas.

The Lausanne Movement's Ministry Collaboration Network is working toward the goal of reaching the whole world with the whole gospel. The statement says,

> God has designed the Body of Christ to work together, and when we do, he pours out his blessing to bring life forevermore (Ps 133). Kingdom collaboration has proven to reduce duplication of effort, maximize Kingdom resources, and bring diverse groups together to solve complex problems that cannot be addressed by individual organizations.
>
> We envision a future where every ministry is working in unity with others to accomplish God's mission; where Global North and South are effectively partnering, resources and credit are shared, and mission strategies are jointly developed so the whole gospel can go to the whole world.[31]

We would not survive without the other; we need each other.

Tan writes:

> The most common approach of Western mission agencies or pastoral training ministries in Majority World churches is to package a program that local leaders are expected to implement. Often these programs come in the form of training curricula that are given away for free or sold to participants. Funding is provided as long as local leaders stick to the script and meet expectations. Decision making regarding curriculum, finance, and strategy is often limited to top Western leaders and is trickled down to local leaders for implementation.[32]

Collaboration in mission is not only about efficiency:

> It is the strategic and practical outworking of our shared submission to Jesus Christ as Lord. Too often we have engaged in mission in ways that prioritize and preserve our own identities

---

31. Lausanne Movement, "Ministry Collaboration," accessed 30 September 2022, https://lausanne.org/networks/issues/collaboration.
32. Tan, "Understanding Pastoral Leadership," 45.

(ethnic, denominational, theological, etc.), and have failed to submit our passions and preferences to our one Lord and Master. The supremacy and centrality of Christ in our mission must be more than a confession of faith; it must also govern our strategy, practice and unity.[33]

A divided church or training enterprise achieves little in a divided world. The Cape Town Commitment succinctly held that the two aspects of unity in mission are the collaboration of women and men and "the recognition of the missional nature of theological education":

> *Partnering in the body of Christ for unity in mission.* Paul teaches us that Christian unity is a creation of God, based on our reconciliation with God and with one another. We lament the divisiveness of our churches and organizations, because a divided Church has no message for a divided world. Our failure to live in reconciled unity is a major obstacle to authenticity and effectiveness in mission. We commit to *partnership* in global mission. No one ethnic group, nation or continent can claim the exclusive privilege of being the ones to complete the Great Commission. Two specific aspects of unity in mission are the partnership of women and men and the recognition of the missional nature of theological education.[34]

Collaboration is God's design, vision, and commission. Taking on multiple layers of relationships and uncertain outcomes, it might seem impossible. Therefore, we formulate it not depending on human competence, but by yielding to divine wisdom. This is a biblical call, too.

---

33. Lausanne Movement, "Ministry Collaboration," quoting "The Cape Town Commitment" IIF-2.
34. Kevin Smith, "Summary of the Cape Town Commitment," section IIF, Lausanne Movement, 18 March 2011, accessed 30 September 2022, https://lausanne.org/content/summary-of-the-cape-town-commitment.

6

Envisioning Collaboration: A Biblical and Practical Discourse

The Biblical Call for Collaboration

Genuine collaboration is grounded in the Bible. God is its initiator and sustainer, and an active party. In the Bible, the call to extraordinary collaboration involves the giving of oneself, cooperating by giving away the best of one's treasures and privileges, and the giving over of exclusivity claims, all for the kingdom's sake. The culture of independent kingdom-building must be overthrown by a theological commitment to "be one," as Jesus prayed for his people and exemplified through his own model of being one with the Father. This is profoundly practical.

God's promise to Abraham was that through him and his descendants all the nations on earth would come into the realm of God's blessing (Gen 12:1–3); the progression of its fulfillment through biblical history was seen in the responsive affirmation or prayer of his people everywhere: "All the nations you have made will come and worship before you, Lord; they will bring glory to your name" (Ps 86:9); its assured fulfillment is that "at the name of Jesus every knee should bow, in heaven and on earth and under the earth, and every tongue acknowledge that Jesus Christ is Lord, to the glory of God the Father" (Phil 2:10–11); and its climactic celebration will be

> a great multitude that no one could count, from every nation, tribe, people and language, standing before the throne and before

the Lamb. They were wearing white robes and were holding palm branches in their hands. And they cried out in a loud voice:

"Salvation belongs to our God,
who sits on the throne,
and to the Lamb."
(Rev 7:9–10)

God's mission transcends boundaries and encompasses all his people everywhere. Only through collaborative vision and practice will we serve this cause.

The biblical metaphors of "being one body" and "being one" are central to any training collaboration we might imagine. When members of one body collaborate to serve one another for the honor and pleasure of God, he pours out his blessings and life in abundance. Psalm 133:1–3 reads,

How good and pleasant it is
    when God's people live together in unity! . . .
For there the LORD bestows his blessing,
    even life forevermore.

For a collaboration to be sustained and to thrive, it must be vision-driven (not trend-making like the Simon model in Acts 8:18), it must involve sacrificial outcomes (not profit-making like the Lot model in Genesis), and it must be for God's eternal plan for the church and its mission (not about making our names great, the Tower of Babel model). In a world that is warring economically and spiritually for personal rights and privileges, only a biblically driven and Spirit-led vision can guide persons or systems to genuine collaboration. In a recent podcast Lucado remarked, "The church needs the Holy Spirit, not another program or trend."[1] True collaboration is the work of the Holy Spirit, whereby humans become useful tools in the divine will.

---

1. Jessica Lea, "Max Lucado: The Church Needs the Holy Spirit, Not Another Program or Trend," Church Leaders, 12 September 2022, https://churchleaders.com/podcast/433631-max-lucado-church-needs-holy-spirit.html.

Equipping Everyone: The Compelling Biblical Directive

Setting up minimum ideals for the church, Dobbins avows the "Church as a Teacher of Disciples." His three affirmations in this regard are that (1) salvation and education are inseparably related, (2) Christian living and maturing must be learned, and (3) a church should serve as a Christian school: "Church is essentially a school."[2] What if the church's mandate of "equipping everyone" is reenvisioned through the way we do theological education? Every member has intrinsic worth and a vital role to accomplish in God's design; hence everyone needs equipping. Believers (the laity), who are often the "frozen credits and dead capital of the church,"[3] as Kraemer puts it, need to be mobilized into responsive engagement in church and society. The Cape Town Commitment commented sharply on the failure of the church in not taking seriously the need to train the whole people of God for their distinct daily callings along with their callings in the church.[4] God's design through the Scriptures and through history has been a strongly collaborative one, where each person is valued for his or her individuality and at the same time called to serve in unity of purpose. Man and woman in the garden of Eden had to collaborate in life and work to accomplish God's plan in spite of being different; humans with an array of skills and callings had to collaborate to build the tabernacle; disciples had to collaborate to be sent out; and in this same way members of the church should collaborate to accomplish their mission. God himself, as the designer and enabler of collaborations, constantly reminds his people to partner in his eternal directives rather than staying separate, warring over their selfish agendas. Collaboration has been an essential component in realizing God's promises for his people, the Israelites in the Old Testament and the church in the New. Collaborations grew into partnerships and alliances based on the sharing of wills and resources, and strategic treaties. However, whenever purposes shifted, covenants were broken, or selfishness or pride crept in, collaborations failed. Lloyd-Jones stated, "Theological teachers and

---

2. Gaines S. Dobbins, "Translating New Testament Principles into Present-Day Practices," in *Building Better Churches: A Guide to the Pastoral Ministry* (Nashville: Broadman, 1947), 83–98.

3. Hendrick Kraemer, *A Theology of the Laity* (Philadelphia: Westminster, 1975), 66.

4. Lausanne Movement, "The Cape Town Commitment," section IIA-3 and IIF-4, https://lausanne.org/content/ctc/ctcommitment#capetown.

tutors have often been academics who know nothing about church life, who know nothing about handling people, and often, who cannot preach."[5] We need collaboration to pool strengths and overcome flaws.

Collaboration is the way of God. "Let us make mankind in our image, in our likeness" is itself the most compelling statement to establish this. When humans crafted plans of collaboration outside the will of God, they ultimately failed, as in the case of the Tower of Babel, the strategies of Joseph's brothers, the plots of Saul against David, the shrewd networks of Judas Iscariot in the New Testament, the alliances formed against the Lord Jesus, and the worldwide network against the Bible and the church to this day. God's plans are to be accomplished in God's way. The church learned this lesson the hard way in the early centuries. Early church leaders had to ensure that the central place of the church and its mission was not compromised by personal interests, cultural preferences, or moral choices. The same can be said about the call on leaders and trainers today: to make sure mission is accomplished God's way. The Acts account presents a candid picture of how diverse personalities and purposes were able to collaborate on the single aim of building the church. The foundation of their collaboration was laid in prayer, waiting on God, worship, fellowship, sharing, and daringly reaching out by the enabling of the Holy Spirit. In such soil collaboration thrives and matures into solid partnerships.

TE as the "study of God" is often interpreted within its cognitive objectives. "The church" in the profound biblical view is the family of God (not families), the body of Christ (not bodies), and in Ephesians, *ecclesia* appears only in the singular. The plural is used with reference to geographical locations and not the church's existential being. The struggle has been one of tackling the monocentric and monocultural way of doing theology and theological education, where theologizing and theological education methodology assume (imagine) one universal path which is the same for everyone, everywhere, at all times. Describing it as "the systematic aggregate of a set of unchanging propositions," van Engen said, "This monocentric view of doing theology [and TE] dominated not only in the Roman and Eastern churches but the various branches of Protestantism and the Reformation as well. This perspective also

---

5. Martyn Lloyd-Jones, *Training Men for the Ministry Today* (London: London Theological Seminary, 1983), 8.

permeated Protestant missions for over 150 years during the time of colonial missions."[6] The term "whole church" denotes the oneness of this body, clergy and laity, the saint in the sanctuary and the marketplace, the scholar and practitioner, in God's *ecclesia* where every member everywhere is a valued disciple and a responsible stakeholder in mission. This encompasses apostles, prophets, teachers, pastors, evangelists, and everyone else in the family of God – men, women, young, old, children, professionals, business personnel, and so on:

> So Christ himself gave the apostles, the prophets, the evangelists, the pastors and teachers, *to equip his people for works of service, so that the body of Christ may be built up until we all reach unity in the faith and in the knowledge of the Son of God and become mature, attaining to the whole measure of the fullness of Christ.*
> (Eph 4:11–13; emphasis added)

Leadership formation must happen within the solid frame of discipleship formation, and both need to thrive in the milieu of mission formation. As Goheen succinctly states, "The key to a missional congregation will be leaders who are already following Christ in his mission and looking for ways to enable and equip the rest of the congregation to follow him more faithfully as well."[7] The task of education therefore must intentionally foster the learning of all, going beyond the nouns "study" and "science" to active continuous verbs such as "knowing," "loving," "obeying," "following," "worshipping," and "serving." This is ignored or undervalued in our monotype, tunnel-like, detached learning environments, both in the formal and the nonformal. Perry says,

> Whether the steps are large or small, programmatic or around a coffee table, one thing seems to be clear: redeeming a vision for Christian education as a component of holistic discipleship is neither a solely pastoral nor a solely academic task. It's a task for the people of God to undertake together – the single mom with

---

6. Charles E. van Engen, "The Glocal Church: Locality and Catholicity in a Globalizing World," in *Globalized Theology: Belief and Practice in an Era of World Christianity*, eds. Craig Ott and Harold A. Netland (Grand Rapids: Baker Academic, 2007), 173.
7. Michael W. Goheen, *A Light to the Nations: The Missional Church and the Biblical Story* (Grand Rapids: Baker, 2011), 220–21.

her nose in a systematic theology textbook and the college student who comes to the small group for the snacks.[8]

The passages of history show us where and how we have fallen short in acknowledging and responding to the whole church body's educational needs.

The "whole church" mandate is not new; it is the biblical, theological, and educational directive. The ICETE Manifesto II, although without explicit emphasis on church-centered theological education, affirms education as the means to serve the church. It states,

> The Church is sent into the entire world to bring people of all nations into communion with Christ and the fellowship of his disciples. . . . Education is an essential part of this Great Commission and theological education finds its purpose and mission within the framework of this mandate.
>
> Finally, the Church sent by Jesus lives on the promise: "I am with you always, to the very end of the age."[9]

If any sector of education has to carry an inclusive vision, it is theological education, where ideally the apostle Paul's vision in Ephesians 4 of "[the equipping of God's] people for works of service, so that the body of Christ may be built up," should find fulfillment. TE schools train scholar-teachers and priestly leaders, but their training landscape should capture the Pauline vision of Colossians 2:6–7: the grounding and rooting of the whole church in God's word and work. Jesus's method best emulates the principle, in that the Master Teacher proficiently dialogued with the learned sectors and simultaneously set up his teaching platform for everyone else who followed him. He surrounded himself judiciously with critical thinkers and enthusiastic practitioners who represented all walks of life, irrespective of preconditions. Jesus exemplified that the service of the kingdom of God employs everyone in vital roles – small or big – and thus he taught Philip, Nathanael, the Samaritan woman, Mary

---

8. Abby Perry, "Non-Traditional Seminary Students Are Changing the Church," CT Creative Studio, 7 January 2020, accessed 1 October 2022, https://www.christianitytoday.com/partners/higher-education/non-traditional-seminary-students-are-changing-church.html.
9. ICETE, "ICETE Manifesto II" (12 July 2022), http://icete.info/wp-content/uploads/2022/10/ICETE-Manifesto-Restatement-Final-version-July-12-2022-1.pdf.

and Martha, and Zacchaeus. Later, the courageous and thoughtful leaders of the New Testament church emerged from those ordinary disciples whom Jesus had taught and walked with.

The church's two core functions – one focused inward and the other outward – are established in the mission of training. The cycle of discipling and evangelizing (building up and equipping the whole church, and sending them out in mission) is dynamic and ongoing, as is evident in the Great Commission of Matthew 28:18–20. Good theological education underpins all this. "The primary task of the Church is to proclaim the Christian gospel, and theology functions first of all as a test and a corrective to measure the integrity of this proclamation."[10] The workforce needed for the harvest is immense and the time is limited and uncertain. Does this require a paradigmatic change in our approach to TE? Perhaps multiple healthy collaborations and cross-fertilization? Should the TE enterprise be reaching out more, rather than waiting for a few to come in to be trained?

The *Ekballō* Drive

In Matthew 9:38 Jesus says, "Ask the Lord of the harvest, therefore, to send out workers into his harvest field." The Greek word translated as "send out" in this verse is *ekballō*, literally (or figuratively) meaning to eject, cast, expel, or put forth, different from the formal sending of the word *apostello* whereby someone is formally sent with a commission. *Ekballō* here means to force people out, to push people out, with a need or sense of urgency. Why *ekballō*?

Global shifts and local disruptions are pushing us to think in new ways and of new means for training and mission. Churches and missions as we have traditionally seen them have been structurally and culturally shaken by the pandemic. A large number of seminaries and training initiatives in South Asia are confronting the challenge of practical collaboration of the formal and nonformal streams of education as an essential means to cater to the needs in discipleship and leadership training. As one technology professional in TE said,

---

10. Karl Barth, *Church Dogmatics*, 1/1, trans. G. Bromiley (Edinburgh: T&T Clark, 1975), 82–83.

> The COVID-19 pandemic has changed the way people think about learning and teaching. The entire higher education in theology is approached by students differently now. The concept of full-time ministry is growing less popular, and faculty have little control over learners compared with earlier times. Interestingly, the major disconnect in upcoming years will be the one between the older faculty and the younger batch of students. The technological and philosophical gap between the two will be immense and we need to prepare to face this in the future. Many leaders in TE are already wondering about the scope of the younger generation joining theological education and the way they might want to learn theology.

FTE is losing out on student enrollment generally. There are emerging concerns in countries such as India regarding the decline in the number of traditional Christians doing theological education and mission. In the words of the principal of a seminary,

> In the past decades in South India, we had Christian families sending their children for theological education and now that number is coming down. . . . When the new converts come to seminaries and Bible colleges to learn the Bible and know Jesus more deeply, what the syllabi give is critical theories and literary analysis in which many find themselves in utmost confusion. . . . The online approach is rapidly catching attention, but several questions accompany that trend, including the theological focus and personal formation.

The rapidly changing sociopolitical scenario in the nations requires a renewed and more responsive evangelical theological trajectory on matters such as the digital transformation, justice concerns, and debates on sexuality. Theological leadership is being forced to be more responsive to the lived realities of Christians within the functional shifts in the church, such as persecution, poverty, migrant and diaspora issues, discipleship concerns, syncretism, heresies, divisions within evangelicalism, leader deficit, and many more. Even prior to the pandemic seminaries were struggling to survive amid economic instability and the impact of the digital-cultural revolution. While curricular rigidity resisted shifts, including the desirable ones, the system of theological educational in the Majority World has often felt anesthetized toward social exclusion, persecution, poverty, and inadequacies in management. Amid the challenges a number of leading seminaries resorted to institutional restructuring toward the integration of online streaming and consequently took on board more tech-oriented personnel, often at the expense of long-term, senior faculty. This has changed the outlook of TE campuses, from relational-styled, mentoring-oriented environments, to more professional, independent, corporate settings. At the other end, the communities of faith are faced with a more desperate need for trained ministry personnel than ever before. An effective blueprint for training will have every member in the church body actively learning and effectively doing. As Green says,

> The world church is looking for ways to equip all of God's people to fulfil his call to mission in his world. . . . The International Study Group on Theological Education for the Edinburgh 2010 Congress states that educating the whole people of God is a key to mission. In the same year, the Lausanne Movement declared its conviction that we need intensive efforts to train all God's people in whole-life discipleship, which means to live, think, work, and speak from a biblical worldview and with missional effectiveness in every place or circumstance of daily life and work.[11]

For this, a collaborative momentum of training in seminaries, missions, and pastorates seems not only advantageous but inevitable too. An *ekballō* impetus must shape our vision for the future, and we must enhance TE qualitatively and quantitatively. Nonetheless, it is imprudent to wait for hundreds of workers in mission or thousands of students in seminaries, when churches are not growing with new and mature disciples.

---

11. Tim Green, "TEE Looking to the Future," in *TEE in Asia: Empowering Churches, Equipping Disciples*, eds. Hanna-Ruth van Wingerden, Tim Green, and Graham Aylett, ICETE (Carlisle: Langham Global Library, 2021), 257–58.

Capturing *Kairos*: Education "In," "By," "For," and "With" the Church

Kairos denotes a divinely appointed time. Ancient Greeks used the word to refer to the "right, critical, and opportune moment" for a new initiative. Appointed people are to seize the moment, partnering with God in his kingdom plans. All our (God-given) resources, institutions, and initiatives are required to serve this God-momentum, willfully yielding other agendas. Historical, sociological, and technological shifts invite us today to reenvision the way we perceive and practice theological education. With the current scenario of conventional models or training initiatives failing to achieve the intended impact in mission, we must face up to the option to humbly and critically revisit our goals and structures. The shift between hemispheres in Christianity's center of gravity, the impact of globalization, the digital transition, the static or shrinking growth of Christianity, and the impact of all of these on TE, point us toward the church. These cultural waves oblige educators and trainers to reckon with new problems, new needs, new prospects, and new challenges that can inform how we equip the church in its life and mission today. At the 2022 Asia Theological Association General Assembly Poobalan discussed the explosive growth of the gospel movement in the Majority World and the threats that are associated with it in the dimensions of faith and behavior. For him, both areas require of us a renewed commitment to radical discipleship that reflects a nondualistic, integral understanding of Christian living and serving in this age.[12] *Kairos* is often marked by enormous challenges and obstacles, but comes with a constraining invitation for the "called out" to respond in unison, in order for the situation to improve. Christians in South Asia need to grapple with their ecclesial and missional status in the present and the future. Before "collaborating" we need clear perspectives, compelling values, and contagious goals.

Hedlund's "fourteen lessons every church must know" seem relevant in this discourse. For him,

- Mission is possible! Whether in a post-modern culture or a hostile environment.

---

12. Dr. Ivor Poobalan, "Plenary 4: The Landscape of Witness and Discipleship in the Digital Age," ATA General Assembly, Penang, 26–30 September 2022, Asia Theological Association, "Plenary Sessions" (2022), https://www.ataasia.com/2022ataga/plenary-sessions/.

- Churches need not be tied to the patterns of the past.
- Christian ministry is for all the members.
- Training for ministry takes place in the local church.
- Leaders are born in the local church.
- Pastors should be trainers of people for the work of ministry.
- Christian mission is the movement of the laity.
- Urbanization offers tremendous scope for Christian mission.
- Cell groups are a primary means of mission in the urban world.
- The Gospel has power to transform lives and society.
- "A church of the poor" can be "a church with power" for witness and service.
- A witnessing church can have a powerful impact in the society.
- Theology should respond to local cultural beliefs and fears.
- Theologians are needed who will exegete both scripture and culture.[13]

Unless some of the old baggage we are carrying (as discussed in the earlier sections) that keeps us from thinking afresh and being responsive is shaken off, a fresh reenvisioning may not emerge. Collaboration of the spectrums of TE should advance the capacity of the church to equip all its people, in the church, by the church, with the church, and for the church. The leadership deficit seems to be a high priority for the church in these changing sociopolitical times. Let us review how the approach of the Regional Training Hubs (RTH) model could address the issue on multiple fronts.

Regional Training Hubs: Ongoing Formation in Discipleship and Leadership

For too long we have revolved around the question of how sectors in TE will unite, and how quality requirements and such a collaboration of initiatives within the spectrum of TE can advance the capacity of the church to equip all its people, *in the church, by the church, with the church, and for the church*, so that from the church, God's mission might flourish in the world. The "symbiotic

---

13. Roger E. Hedlund, "Critique of Pentecostal Mission by a Friendly Evangelical," *Asian Journal of Pentecostal Studies* 8, no. 1 (2005): 94.

paradigm" (see figure 5.3) was formulated in anticipation of FTE and NFTE collaborating with each other and hence strengthening churches and mission organizations. However, the research undertaken, and the review of the paradigm, seem to warrant a shift in focus in the way we approach the issue. It was observed that in the South Asia region reciprocity between FTE and NFTE will tend to be minimal, if it happens at all, and therefore the concern is the edifying and enabling of the church. As theological educators and ministry trainers, what could we do toward thoroughly equipping the church in faith and mission? What kind of collaboration will produce an outcome that can keep the church fervent in mission, as in the book of Acts? What is blocking us from catalyzing a combined momentum where FTE, NFTE, Christian NGOs, and mission organizations serve the church and its mission, particularly in the areas of solid discipleship and leadership development? See figure 6.1 for diagrammatic depictions of these ideas.

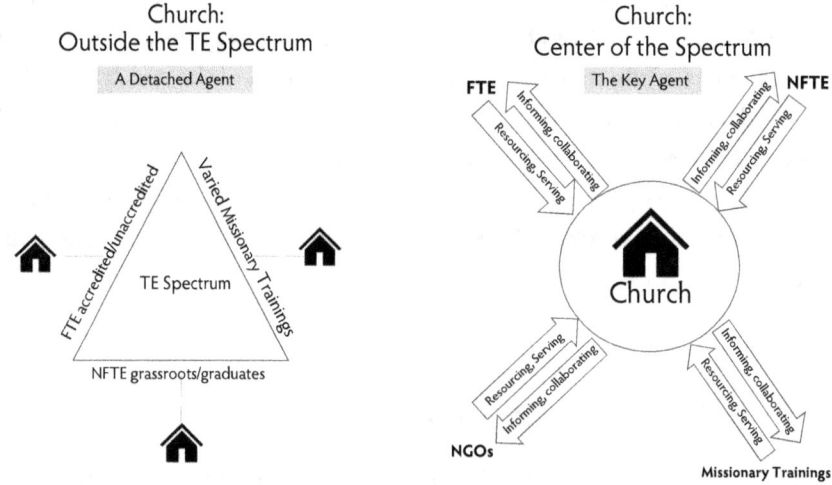

Figure 6.1 Depiction of Church Positioning in TE

The landscape of TE must change for the growth of Christianity in today's world. The most powerful alliance will be one in which theological institutions give themselves for the benefit of the life and mission of the church near them. This assumes drastic shifts and movements; it will require much from all of us at multiple levels, yet the vision of the kingdom of God is worth it. It calls both the church and the seminary to genuine humility and authentic action. Regional Training Hubs (RTH) is a training design that offers a promising and resolute vision to address the problem.

The RTH paradigm aims to tackle concerns such as TE's increasing detachment as a separate entity from the church, the neglect of ongoing disciple-making and missional formation in the church, scholars' detachment from the church and evangelistic mission, the lack of church-oriented outcomes in theological education, institutions straying from their missional goals, graduates not returning to serve the local contexts/churches, elitist divides in academic communities, the pressure on ordinary learners to adjust their identity, language obstacles and resulting inefficiency, lack of accountability and quality checks, and ministry placement issues.

The "Hub"

A "hub" denotes the central part of a circular object; in a training program, it is the "center of learning and action." It is the central connection point which holds multiple elements stably around it. This hub must hold the collaborating array of institutions or initiatives to serve the compelling range of its mission. The Regional Training Hubs model is designed to serve this purpose.

The Regional Training Hubs (RTH) is a strategic regional partnership of training institutions and personnel who by ongoing contextual learning and dependency on God envision the forward trajectory of the church and facilitate national collaborators in equipping every believer in life and service. Hubs are networks promoting and catalyzing research, interactions, collaboration, connections, relationships, and exploration. RTH is not intended to be a "training provider," a "new program deliverer," or "a super institution," as people might assume; rather, it represents a team consisting of experienced equippers and strategists across the spectrum of TE who attentively listen and strategically assist the dynamic constituencies in the context of the church. RTH galvanizes the collaboration of various agencies such as global partners, national collaborators, regional catalysts, local facilitators, and resource coordinators, and enables church-centered learning to be put into action.

There should be country-based operational networks of facilitators and resource developers within local churches or local church networks in areas where discipleship, leadership, and missional formation are notably scarce.

RTHs engage in ongoing ground surveys, collaborations, innovation, and transformative learning designs with and for the church, and concurrently enhance collaborative training and mission initiatives with seminaries, NGOs, and mission training institutions. RTH facilitates the service of countrywide initiatives and sees that churches are flourishing in quality and quantity across the land.

The Church as the Central Agent and Key Stakeholder of Training

Drawing on the discussions and study above, we recognize the need to locate the "center" of our training mission. It is the church, as all the literary, historical, and biblical directives point to. The disadvantageous gap in training has always been associated with having the church sidelined as one of the stakeholders, and not as *the main agent* or *the center*. In this, the church has no battle with either the formal or the nonformal. The biblical design has positioned the church at the center; all we need is a reenvisioning and reaffirming of the same.

Figure 6.2 Church-Centered Regional Training Hubs Model

Distinct Features of Regional Training Hubs (RTH) South Asia

- *Location:* RTH is not another organization or academic program; rather, it is a resource team comprised of committed visionary leaders from across the TE sectors, serving churches at their points of need in training. RTH will primarily focus on isolated and neglected churches that function with significantly little scope for ongoing discipleship, leadership, and mission-engagement education.
- *Collaboration:* RTHs are unique in their vision for "breakthrough collaboration" realized with the active participation of trainers in the formal, nonformal, and informal, mission agencies, and NGOs rendering service to the local church base. The motto is "Listening, Learning, Leveraging." The RTH model will also make sure seminaries and mission trainings are enhanced by "creative internships," "co-teaching," "learning resource development," and "shared evaluation."
- *Formation:* Contextual and integral formation are key motifs, where every member in the church, irrespective of age, gender, class, or education level, assumes a significant place in education and service. The practical outworking of this model and its quality assurance format will be developed in the following phase of context-based, region-specific research.
- *Learning approach:* Different from the traditional track of siloed courses that exclude or considerably limit biblical literacy, theological wisdom, and mission engagement in local communities, RTHs creatively engage people in the ongoing design of learning and the continuity of learning through relevant engagement in mission and leadership, thereby advancing local ownership of mission and church growth.
- *Participation:* The South Asian paradigm of RTH envisages that "all-level discipleship," "all-level leadership," and "all-level mission engagement" formation is made available to every Christian to appreciate and live out his or her vocation to the full. Leadership and mission engagement are built within the frame of discipleship, where persons are spiritually formed in the church community.

- *Contribution:* The key beneficiary of RTH is the church on the ground. Its worship and witness base are strengthened by equipping all members in the Word. It provides churches with concrete support to stand firm and move on with trained leadership who can navigate through change and continue equipping their people in their own preferred ways of learning and serving.

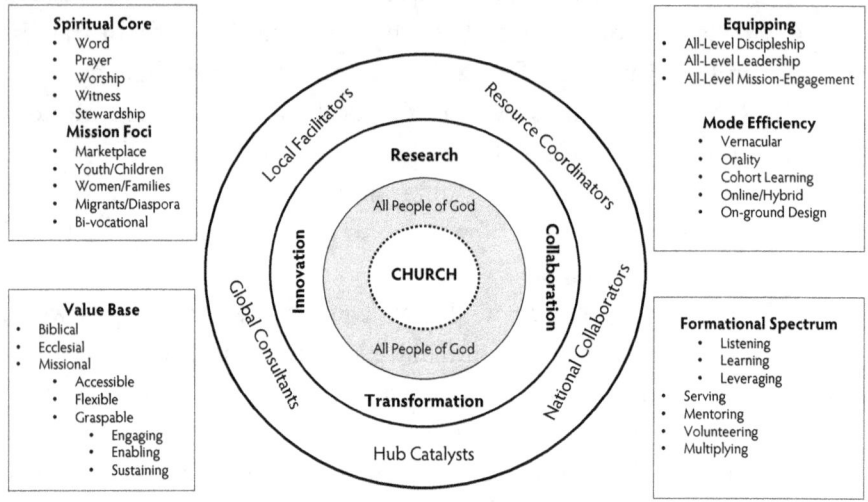

Figure 6.3 Regional Training Hubs (RTH): Philosophy and Function

The RTH serves church-centered training through a network of the following:

Global Consultants

These are the visionary leaders, experienced in the context of the church's mission in South Asia, who can share insights on the collaborative prospects of training sectors in the region and on the value of sustainable regional ownership of the mission of the hub. Global consultants may contribute to the thinking process, while not necessarily being responsible for the practical functioning of the hub.

National Collaborators

These are the national leaders who can aid local momentum whenever assistance is required with training needs or learning resources. National collaborators could be immediate supports to local initiatives. Both global consultants and national collaborators will be more of a background yet strategic presence in RTH.

Hub Catalysts

This is the resource team with country representatives from South Asian nations committed to see the region thriving in mission and church planting through meaningful collaborations across the spectrum of TE. The catalysts stand in the middle with their twofold commitment: (1) to listen to global consultants and national collaborators, and (2) to learn from local facilitators and resource coordinators and leverage the "equipping ground" of the church. This team ensures that genuine collaboration happens in two ways: through building up churches to strengthen their own training base, and building bridges to strengthen seminaries and mission training centers to develop a holistic vision. The hub catalysts will identify and mobilize those who share the values and resources of church-focused TE representing the formal, nonformal, Christian NGOs, and the marketplace mission. This is the team supporting the church to reenvision its training dimensions and help it to own the responsibility of the ongoing equipping of members.

Local Facilitators

These are the multilevel equippers in local churches or church networks who engage simultaneously in ongoing learning and ongoing training in the church. They are the functional educators and trainers in the church who work closely with hub catalysts and resource coordinators and give them clarity on learning styles, needs, challenges, and preferences. The research outcomes pointed to the significance of three foundational dimensions, namely discipleship, leadership, and mission engagement, and facilitators will be equipped for this task. Held in balance, this threefold equipping can make churches flourish; not including all three dimensions would incapacitate mission and leader development.

Resource Coordinators

This team is critical in the frame of RTH in analyzing the church's needs in discipleship, leadership, and missional engagement alongside the local facilitators. Regional coordinators will explore the type of learning and learning levels and resources that suit the context to assist the service of the local facilitators. Training contexts that are rich in learning resources may not fully understand the challenges of education in scarce-resource contexts.

RTH Functional Method

The RTH resource team provides overall support in realizing a collaborative momentum across the theological education spectrum for the advantage of local churches or church networks. The ways in which the church will be central to the hub will be determined by the local dynamics, needs, and prospects. Context-based research on the needs, challenges, and opportunities of the church will shape the function of the hub. Church leaders will join hands with the FTE-NFTE facilitators who have embraced a renewed ecclesial vision in training and the church will assume the central role in defining and directing the missional goal of the hub.

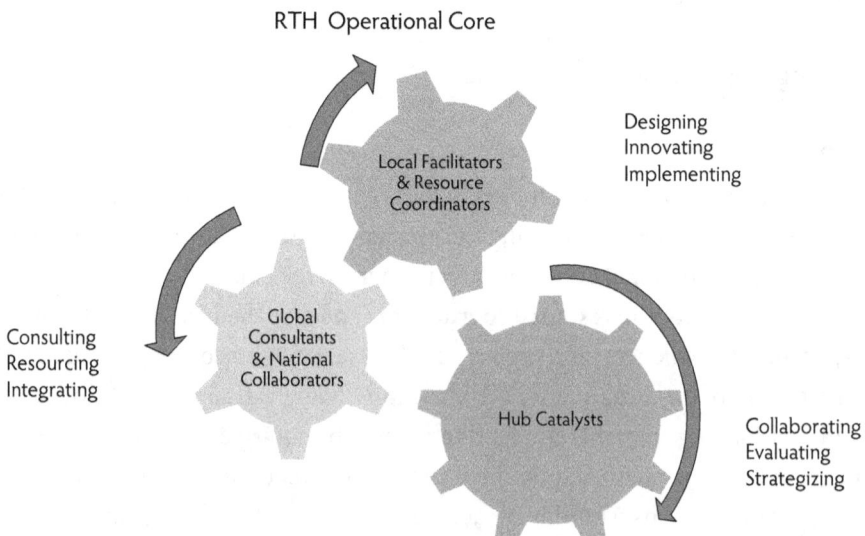

Figure 6.4 Church-Centered Hub Operations

Envisioning Collaboration: A Biblical and Practical Discourse

Innovating and endeavoring to create sustainable momentum is the goal. "Continuity streams to equip all the people of God" is a key feature of the vision. Hub catalysts in consultation with the RTH facilitate collaboration, research, and innovation for and with the church.

RTH Missional Foci

With the objectives of reaching in, reaching out, and collaborating, the RTH commits to strengthening the base of local church communities. Each of the foci is strategic and will resolve the church's need for stability and sustainability in the region.

Figure 6.5 RTH Missional Thrust

The interworking of these components and the quality and sustainability of the procedures in the RTH model are beyond the scope of this project. This prospect will be explored further and crystalized at the next level of the study, undertaken through a countrywide prototype approach. This study prefers listening and facilitating over prescribing and packaging.

To recapitulate, this study has affirmed how learning of all kinds is taking place significantly through formal seminaries and nonformal programs, each having its own niche and contribution to make in the region of South Asia. While we uphold the vital role being played by seminaries and nonformal institutions, we have also seen unfavorable dissonances in the philosophy and practice of TE. Existential appreciation and critical checks of the formal and nonformal streams need to be held in balance. Historically, TE in the region has shifted its locus from the church to seminary campuses, and nonformal programs have flourished in taking training to where people are; more recently, TE has been creatively negotiating with the massive digital transformation in the post-pandemic season. In the training triangle (seminaries, NFTE programs, and missionary institutes), churches have in many places become an outside agency with limited influence and involvement. From being the cradle of discipleship and mission formation, churches eventually handed theology and theological education over to the seminaries, which eventually became *the agents* of formal theological education, while on the other side, mission agencies developed their own training patterns to meet their ongoing need for workers. As the gaps steadily widened over time, churches in many places became indifferent or dissatisfied about formal seminary education and started distancing themselves further from an active role in any of their endeavors. Seminaries turned into settings of elite academic inquiry, growing less relevant to the changing realities on the ecclesial and missional ground in the nations.

Along with the plight of disconnect from the church and the disintegration of formal and nonformal forms, there has been a growing awareness of a need for reenvisioning TE in the region. The Global Leadership Challenge and the status of the Christian population in many places point to the enormous need for responsive training to keep churches flourishing in quality and quantity. Sociopolitical situations in the region also warrant solid collegiality and interdependence among the training sectors. With all this in mind, ideally we imagine living authentically in the ecclesial ecosystem, where souls are added to the church, seeds are securely formed on the seedbed of the seminary, and are replanted in churches and mission fields with stronger roots to serve efficiently.

If the FTE-NFTE symbiotic paradigm is contextually feasible, it is time to put energy and resources into it. Otherwise, we are warned to think beyond the classical, conventional prerogatives to seek ways in which the training sectors should channel their efforts and resources for the benefit of the church and its mission.

From surveying the literature, we have sensed that Christianity has arrived at a *kairos* given the shifting of its center of gravity in the hemispheres, the impact of globalization and global crises on the TE momentum, and the vigorous dialogues on FTE-NFTE collaboration, among other factors. As individuals and institutions, we are obliged to respond to this moment in history when, as in the Acts of the Apostles, the Word must be spread, and Christianity must flourish in the region with significant outward expansion. It is also essential to have corrective measures to grapple with the lopsided theology pushing the church to the fringes and separating theological wisdom and missional formation from its agenda. With the complexities of social exclusion, chronic poverty, persecution, and religious fanaticism in South Asia, theological grounding cannot be parted from practical evangelism and church planting. As *one body*, all training entities are summoned to serve the church to prepare it as the focal agent of God's mission in a hurting, sinful world. This requires humility, discernment, sacrifice, and selfless sharing of the treasured claims or resources on the part of every training sector. This prospect requires strategic partnerships and initiatives, all driven by the biblical, missional, and prophetic mandate. We maintain that kingdom values are realized only when strengths are shared, claims harmonized, resources given over, and eternity envisioned. The hard shells of the long-preserved tendencies of particularizing how to do theology in global and local settings must be broken and we must start afresh by "listening, learning, and leveraging" in favor of churches in the land. Hence a recentering of theological and missional formation to its original ground, that is, the church, emerges decisively. This central agent is the ideal beneficiary of the partnerships envisioned. In other words, the church shifts from being one of the stakeholders to being the key agent of all educational and formative endeavors. Acceleration of global evangelization and attainment of biblically driven social engagement are the outcomes of the theological-hermeneutical community in the church.

Exploring potential collaborations of the formal and nonformal sectors projected the question of "quality" in training as the core issue, and it is undeniably a matter of importance to the enterprise. While the formal needs to improve its practice by addressing its need for a more holistic and transformative education, the nonformal could improve by achieving a deeper theological grounding and a foundation of quality assurance. However, from the survey of the literature and global consultations and listening to the context of South Asian TE, it has come to light that the central issue even in determining "quality" is about TE's premediated goal of serving the church. Ideally, FTE and NFTE maintain the same goal – at best they are supposed to – that is, building the church into maturity for the coming of the Lord. Collaborations that lead to this end, as the study proposes, will be possible only by listening and building relationships across the spectrum of TE. While "quality assurance" raises a significant and immediate prospect, the ultimate pursuit must be the church's equipping as God's agent of mission in this world. The future of theological education is in listening and building relationships between visionary educators committed to upholding the cause of the church by equipping and engaging local believers.

Centuries of appeals to theological education to be responsive and innovative for the cause of the church have dynamically re-emerged in the past few years driven by varied forces, including the pandemic. The vision of collaboration goes far beyond temporary fixes and occasional events; it is a dynamic, flexible, and bottom-up momentum. Perhaps the most challenging aspect is the unpredictability of the trajectory, which we see as the God-space that keeps beckoning our obedience and dependency. From time to time we must critically review how rigid goal-setting and blind adherence to predictability in our actions sometimes moves God easily out of the scheme. Transferring the vision's outline to a blueprint takes prayerful collaboration, risk-taking, and ongoing listening in local contexts.

Right questions are great motivators and change-agents. They source correction and creativity. Praying with other people and churches often defines the direction and takes things further organically. Collaboration is not to be forced. We only prayerfully prepare a vision-driven environment to see God stirring hearts toward that end, because we are catalyzing change in human lives, not in constructs. The prerequisite for genuine collaboration is a compelling vision. And we recognize that the church is that captivating vision, to which no programs or structures can compare.

The listening process has made the study shift focus from the concerns over resolving technical problems or collaborating systems in TE to the equipping of every believer in faith and service. Beyond the focuses of earning credibility or endowing credentials, which are undeniably vital, we must value the building up of every believer and think how this could be done creatively and spiritually in the rapidly shifting landscape of the world. "Irrigating the whole land" is central to the call. As discussed earlier, an end-to-end dripping hose must shape our thinking in this regard. The answer lies in getting all members of the church to do their part in their own circles of interaction and influence across the strata of the society; this was the biblical pattern, and this will be the future direction of mission. These thoughts have been shaped into the model of a Regional Training Hubs vision in South Asia facilitating the growth momentum. In this, the church and church networks are served by a hub catalyst team who are equippers of facilitators, formed within the church, and belonging to varied TE sectors. Technically, this team would align multiple resource agents from across the training spectrum to make churches thrive in internal life and outward mission. As one research participant remarked, the most urgent need is for the maintenance of a substantial amount of salt to give the taste of God's truth to our lands and to preserve our generation from further spiritual and ethical deterioration. In this, a Sunday school child, a teenager, a young mother, or a professional is as significant as a renowned theologian or professional member of the clergy in his or her own circles of relations and influence. There is no "right" way to collaborate to this end; collaborations that impact eternity evolve when they are God-initiated, Spirit-enabled, and willingly undertaken.

Closing Remarks

The changing landscape of education and Christian engagement warrants a critical reenvisioning of our philosophy and practice of theological education. For TE endeavors to have committed learners, obviously the churches must grow in sound health and strategic vision. Strengthening the base thus strengthens the building. The church is not a competitor to any other institution; its central place and missional vitality are uniquely and spiritually bestowed. The urgent task, therefore, is to enable the church theologically and spiritually to move from the margins to assume its central space in theological and missional formation. Conserving the DNA of the church as the body of Christ in the world is God's work in which teachers and trainers across the spectrum should willingly partner. From the literary and field data, we contend that mere structural constructs or conventionalities will not help the church in South Asia thrive in the coming decades. In closing, we reaffirm the following points:

- Unless the church on the ground benefits from formal, nonformal, and informal training, we will end up building great structures on shaky foundations.
- Wherever the goal of serving the church is not attended to or is moved out to the periphery, theological education, regardless of its form, becomes an aimless pursuit.
- We need relational collaborations that blend theological conviction, persuasive generosity, solid reciprocity, and authentic humility in building the *ecclesia* in all-level discipleship, all-level leadership, and all-level mission and social engagement.
- We are coming to a collectively prompting *kairos* – a moment to venture into uncharted pathways of church-centered, church-oriented collaboration. There is nothing predictable, yet for the body and the bride of Christ we hope this momentum will unfold at its own pace and in its own shape and contextual will.

Finally, and most importantly, this study is just a beginning. It does not aim to generalize an agenda or conclude with a proposal; rather, it seeks to establish the significance of polycentric listening and relationship-oriented collaborations for a church-centered collaborative model of theological education. The RTH paradigm will be crystalized and distilled in the South Asian mission soil toward bringing training back to the church by a collaborative input of training streams across theological education. This compelling vision will gain its momentum by *action research* in which RTH's countrywide prototypes will be concurrently implemented, evaluated, and improved to see leadership deficits resolved and Christianity thrive in the region of South Asia.

Appendix 1

Defining Formal and Nonformal TE

Author: Marvin Oxenham, PhD Hybrid
Consultation 2021 Resources – ICETE

One problem in the dialogue between "formal" and "nonformal" theological education is the lack of clear and agreed boundary lines to distinguish them. In reality, programs usually sit on a matrix that combines different approaches. The chart below suggests a set of categories that range from nonformal to formal. It is offered as a tool for analysis, planning, and dialogue, and to define a program. For each category, place an "X" where the program fits in the spectrum and determine in which categories a program is formal and/or nonformal.

Category	Diagnostic question	Scores				
		NONFORMAL		↔		FORMAL
Quantity	How many hours are necessary to complete the program?	5–20	21–100	101–300	301–1000	>1000

Category	Diagnostic question					
Duration	How long does the program last?	Open	1–5 weeks	6–12 weeks	13–52 weeks	>52 weeks

Category	Diagnostic question					
Level	Describe the study level of the program.	Elementary	Basic	Intermediate	High	Advanced

Category	Diagnostic question	Scores				
		NONFORMAL		↔		**FORMAL**
Difficulty	How difficult is the program to complete?	Very easy	Easy	Intermediate	Challenging	Very challenging
Outcomes	How would you describe the program outcomes?	Strongly practical	Mostly practical	Mix of practical and theoretical	Mostly theoretical	Strongly theoretical
Learning activities	How would you describe content of learning activities?	Entirely on the field	Mostly on the field	Mix of field and classroom	Mostly classroom	Entirely in the classroom
Proximity relation	To whom does the program relate?	The church	Mostly the church	Mix of church and academy	Mostly scholarly academy	The scholarly academy
Immediate relevance	How long does it take until graduates apply what they've learned?	Immediately	Relatively soon	Some soon and some later	Mostly later	Application is visible long-term
Delivery in context	Do students need to relocate for the program?	Not at all	A few times	50% of the time	Most of the time	All of the time
Access	How easily can the target audience access the program?	Very easy	Easy	Intermediate	Challenging	Very challenging

Defining Formal and Nonformal TE

Category	Diagnostic question	Scores				
		NONFORMAL		↔		**FORMAL**
Entry	What qualifications are needed to enter the program?	None	Very few	Some	Significant	Strict
Assessment	How is assessment of learning managed?	No assessment	Very loosely	Intermediate	Clear demands	High demands
Accreditation	Is there a form of external quality management?	None	Informal, trust-based	Organizational level	Higher education level	National degree level
Certification	Do students receive certification of learning?	None	Informally	Organizational certification	A formal qualification	A higher education degree
Curriculum	Is there a curriculum to follow?	None	Selections of options	Mix of options and core	Fixed curriculum with few options	Rigid core curriculum

Appendix 2

Opinionnaire 1

Respondents:
Lead Trainers/ Experienced Faculty in Theological Education (TE)
(40 respondents selected from four South Asian countries – 10 each)

[This Opinionnaire is part of Jessy Jaison's research project done in partnership with the UWM-OC ministry[1] and Dallas Theological Seminary. On this form, *formal theological education (FTE)* represents traditional seminary/Bible school education with academic credentialing, and *nonformal theological education (NFTE)* stands for other forms of training, where the purpose is primarily ministry skills development. Please type your answers after each question. Thank you!]

Your name:_____
Name & place of your mission agency/church/NGO:_____
Number of years you have been in training ministry:_____
Average number of persons you train annually in your country:
FTE:_____ NFTE:_____

1. How are most of the church planting and growth endeavors in your country happening?
    - Through the work of graduates from Bible schools and seminaries
    - By trainees from nonformal, short-term, field-based, or church-based programs
    - Both equally
    - Any other:_____

---

1. United World Mission (UWM) is a global mission agency focusing on equipping leaders and establishing churches. Overseas Council (OC) is a ministry of UWM that strengthens the work of partner schools around the globe through its Regional Directors and training initiatives like the Institute of Excellence.

2. A recent study reported, "90% of pastors and church/mission leaders have no or little theological training." Is this true in your country? _____ YES/NO. Expand your answer.
3. If "Yes," what could be factors hindering emerging leaders from getting trained in the seminaries/Bible colleges?
4. Write down 3–4 top teaching needs in your context (name the courses or programs most needed) to accelerate church planting and leader development in your country.
5. What could be the reasons that keep traditional seminaries sometimes at a distance from the NFTE initiatives in your country?
6. Do you think it will be good if the FTE and NFTE streams in your country can collaborate? _____ YES/NO. How/Why? Please expand your answer.
7. Critics say that generally NFTE initiatives fail to keep quality standards, since they do not follow standard structures or external assessments. For situations where this is true, please suggest specific ways to set quality assurance for NFTE.
8. While designing/developing NFTE trainings, what should be the common quality standards you would recommend for your nation?
9. What specific ways would you suggest to bring churches, mission organizations, and seminaries together to serve the immense leadership training needs in your region?

Are there any other things you would like to share about theological education and ministry training in your nation?

Appendix 3

Opinionnaire 2

Respondents:
Key Educators/Strategists in Theological Education (TE)
(10 key leaders selected from educational training initiatives in South Asia)

[This Opinionnaire is part of Jessy Jaison's research project done in partnership with the UWM-OC ministry[1] and Dallas Theological Seminary. On this form, *formal theological education (FTE)* represents traditional seminary/Bible school education with academic credentialing, and *nonformal theological education (NFTE)* stands for other forms of education provided by churches/missions, where often the goal is multilevel skills development for ministry. Please type your answer in clear points after each question. Thank you!]

Your name:_____
Name of your mission agency/church/NGO:_____
Number of years you have been in the ministry of education/training:_____
Average number of persons you train annually in South Asia:
FTE:_____ NFTE:_____

1. From your long-term training experience in South Asia, do you think an authentic, ongoing collaboration between FTE and NFTE is possible? _____ (YES/NO/MAYBE). How/Why? (Please expand your answer.)

---

[1]. United World Mission (UWM) is a global mission agency focusing on equipping leaders and establishing churches. Overseas Council (OC) is a ministry of UWM that strengthens the work of partner schools around the globe through its Regional Directors and training initiatives like the Institute of Excellence.

2. If you were asked to come up with specific recommendations whereby FTE and NFTE could efficiently collaborate to serve each other in your country, what could be those meeting points?
3. Do you think that formal accreditation for NFTE will resolve the FTE-NFTE tension? _____ (YES/NO/MAYBE). How/Why?
4. In contexts where formal accreditation is less preferred or not feasible for NFTE, what do you think are alternative ideas to get such training initiatives validated?
5. In your opinion, what should be the common standards/steps of quality assurance for the countless NFTE initiatives in South Asia?
6. What are practical ways you would suggest to bring churches, mission organizations, and seminaries together for the wide-ranging leadership training needs in South Asia?

Are there any other things you would like to share about theological education and ministry training in your context?

Appendix 4

Respondents – Opinionnaires 1 & 2

Respondents' Name Code	#Years in Ministry	Annual #Students FTE	Annual #Students NFTE
LTF 1	36	18	560
LTF 2	23	0	300
LTF 3	22	0	300
LTF 4	25	0	20
LTF 5	25	50	100
LTF 6	23	0	10
LTF 7	22	25	1500
LTF 8	24	0	50
LTF 9	20	25	60
LTF 10	41	100	200
LTF 11	20	0	175
LTF 12	8	30	0
LTF 13	19	0	100
LTF 14	8	90	120
LTF 15	25	85	350
LTF 16	22	18	15
LTF 17	20	100	100
LTF 18	25	12	350
LTF 19	27	50	100
LTF 20	11	50	20
LTF 21	7	30	70
LTF 22	18	18	0

LTF 23	18	250	500
LTF 24	10	0	1000
LTF 25	8	50	100
LTF 26	15	85	1000
LTF 27	20	0	5000
LTF 28	32	160	550
LTF 29	25	150	50
LTF 30	28	250	700
LTF 31	5	90	100
LTF 32	22	150	50
RTS#1/JZ	20	400	15000
RTS#2/IY	29	30	140
RTS#3/HX	35	380	250
RTS#4/GW	15	0	200
RTS#5/FV	26	700	0
RTS#6/EU	20	90	100
RTS#7/DT	42	0	15000
RTS#8/CS	20	30	100
RTS#9/BR	42	0	300
RTS#10/AQ	35	250	1000

Bibliography

Alpha USA. https://alphausa.org.

Armstrong, Jonathan J. "Extending the Reach of the Traditional Seminary Classroom." Report of Session A, Open Dialogue Summary. The Global Proclamation Congress for Pastoral Trainers, Bangkok, Thailand, June 2016. Revised Summary, September 2016.

Asian Access https://www.asianaccess.org

Asia Theological Association. "Plenary Sessions." 2022. https://www.ataasia.com/2022ataga/plenary-sessions/.

Athyal, Saphir. "Missiological Core of Theological Education" *UBS Journal*, vol.1 no.2, September 2003.

Banks, Robert. *Re-envisioning Theological Education: Exploring a Missional Alternative to Current Models*. Grand Rapids: Eerdmans, 1999.

Barth, Karl. *Church Dogmatics*, 1/1. Translated by G. Bromiley. Edinburgh: T&T Clark, 1975.

BILD International. https://bild.org.

Bolsinger, Tod. *Canoeing the Mountains: Christian Leadership in Uncharted Territory*. Downers Grove: InterVarsity Press 2015.

Bonfiglio, Ryan P. "It's Time to Rethink Our Assumptions about Where Theological Education Happens." *The Christian Century*. 13 February 2019. https://www.christiancentury.org/article/opinion/it-s-time-rethink-our-assumptions-about-where-theological-education-happens.

Bosch, David. "Theological Education in Missionary Perspective." *Missiology* 10, no. 1 (1982): 13–34.

Bruce, L., M. Aring, and B. Brand. "Informal Learning: The New Frontier of Employee & Organizational Development." *Economic Development Review* 15, no. 4 (1998): 12–18.

Burke, David, Richard Brown, and Qaiser Julius. "Challenges Facing Contemporary Theological Education and the Case for TEE." In *TEE for the 21st Century*, edited by David Burke, Richard Brown, and Qaiser Julius, 17–43. ICETE. Carlisle: Langham Global Library, 2021.

Butler, Phill. "Characteristics of High-Performance Ministry Networks." Synergy Commons, 2 January 2014. Accessed 30 September 2022. https://synergycommons.net/resources/characteristics-of-high-performance-ministry-networks/.

Campbell, Heidi. *When Religion Meets New Media*. Abingdon: Routledge, 2010.
Cannell, Linda. "A Review of Literature on Distance Education." *Theological Education* 36, no. 1 (1999): 1–72.
———. *Theological Education Matters: Leadership Education for the Church*. Newburg: EDCOT, 2006.
Cardenas, David. "Viewing Missional Collaboration as an Ecosystem." *Mission Frontiers*, 1 May 2020. Accessed 30 September 2022. https://www.missionfrontiers.org/issue/article/viewing-missional-collaboration-as-an-ecosystem.
Chrispal, Ashish. "Theological Education: Which Way?" In *Be Focused . . . Use Common Sense . . . Overcome Excuses and Stupidity*, edited by Reuben van Rensburg, Zoltan Erdey, and Thomas Schirrmacher, 177–83. Bonn: Verlag für Kultur und Wissenschaft, 2022.
Clark, David K. *To Know and Love God: Method for Theology*. Wheaton: Crossway, 2003.
Coe, Shoki. "Theological Education: A Worldwide Perspective." *Theological Education*, Autumn 1974.
Collinson, Sylvia Wilkey. *Making Disciples*. Milton Keynes: Paternoster, 2004.
Conner, Marica. "Informal Learning: Developing a Value for Discovery." In *Leading Organizational Learning: Harnessing the Power of Knowledge*, edited by Marshall Goldsmith, Howard Morgan, and Alexander J. Ogg. San Francisco: Jossey-Bass, 2004.
"Converging Streams? Thinking about Non-Formal and Formal Pastoral Formation in Dialogue." Leadership Development Consultation (LDC). Chiang Mai, Thailand. 24 May 2017.
Crizaldo, Rei Lemuel. "Asian Theologians Consider the Digital Turn in Education." Report from the 2022 Triennial Assembly of the Asia Theological Association (ATA), Penang, September 2022. *WEA Theological News* 51, no. 4 (Oct. 2022): 2.
Crowley, Michael. "Study by Extension for All Nations." In *Ministry by the People*, edited by F. Ross Kinsler, 42–51. Maryknoll: Orbis, 1983.
Cunningham, Scott. "Innovation in Seminary Theological Education: An Overview of Contributing Forces." In *Be Focused . . . Use Common Sense . . . Overcome Excuses and Stupidity*, edited by Reuben van Rensburg, Zoltan Erdey, and Thomas Schirrmacher, 195–210. Bonn: Verlag für Kultur und Wissenschaft, 2022.
Dallas Theological Seminary. "Training Pastors around the World: Michael A. Ortiz, Ramesh Richard and Darrell L. Bock." A dialogue over how TE is changing in and through the church. YouTube, 5 November 2021. https://www.youtube.com/watch?v=HVhF6khzNq4&t=219s.

Dearborn, Timothy. "Transforming Theological Education through Multi-Institutional Partnerships." In *Christianity and Education: Shaping Christian Thinking in Context*, edited by David Emmanuel Singh and Bernard C. Farr, 33–44. Eugene: Wipf & Stock, 2011.

Dobbins, Gaines S. "Translating New Testament Principles into Present-Day Practices." In *Building Better Churches: A Guide to the Pastoral Ministry*, 83–98. Nashville: Broadman, 1947.

Douglas, Lois McKinney. "Globalizing Theology and Theological Education." In *Globalized Theology: Belief and Practice in an Era of World Christianity*, edited by Craig Ott and Harold A. Netland, 267–87. 2nd printing. Grand Rapids: Baker Academic, 2007.

Farley, Edward. *The Fragility of Knowledge: Theological Education in the Church and University.* Philadelphia: Fortress, 1988.

———. *Theologia: The Fragmentation and Unity of Theological Education.* Philadelphia: Fortress Press, 1983.

Ferris, Robert W. "Accreditation." In *Evangelical Dictionary of World Missions*, edited by A. Scott Moreau. Grand Rapids: Baker, 2000.

"FTE and NFTE in Dialogue." July 2022. http://ecte.eu/wp-content/uploads/2022/09/FTE-and-NFTE-Thematic-Analysis.pdf.

Global Proclamation Commission for Trainers of Pastors. Accessed 18 October 2022. https://gprocommission.org.

Goheen, Michael W. *A Light to the Nations: The Missional Church and the Biblical Story.* Grand Rapids: Baker, 2011.

González, Justo L. "There's No Theological Education Pipeline Anymore." *The Christian Century*, 30 December 2020. Accessed 30 September 2022. https://www.christiancentury.org/article/how-my-mind-has-changed/there-s-no-theological-education-pipeline-anymore.

Gordon-Conwell Seminary. "Frequently Asked Questions." Accessed 6 July 2022. https://www.gordonconwell.edu/center-for-global-christianity/research/quick-facts/.

Green, Tim. "TEE Looking to the Future." In *TEE in Asia: Empowering Churches, Equipping Disciples*, edited by Hanna-Ruth van Wingerden, Tim Green, and Graham Aylett, 257–62. ICETE. Carlisle: Langham Global Library, 2021.

Handley, Joseph W., Jr. *Polycentric Mission Leadership: Toward a New Theoretical Model for Global Leadership.* Oxford: Regnum, 2022.

Hardy, Steven A. *Excellence in Theological Education: Effective Training for Church Leaders.* ICETE. Carlisle: Langham Global Library, 2016.

Hedlund, Roger E. "Critique of Pentecostal Mission by a Friendly Evangelical." *Asian Journal of Pentecostal Studies* 8, no. 1 (2005): 67–94.
Heywood, David. "A New Paradigm for Theological Education?" *Anvil* 17, no. 1 (2000): 19–27.
Hopewell, James F. "The Worldwide Problem: Preparing the Candidate for Mission." In *Theological Education by Extension*, edited by Ralph D. Winter, 36–53. Pasadena: William Carey Library.
Hough, Joseph C., Jr., and John B. Cobb. *Christian Identity and Theological Education*. Atlanta: Scholars, 1985.
ICETE. "Characteristics of Effective and Fruitful Nonformal Theological Education." April 2023. Accessed 18 May 2023. http://icete.info/wp-content/uploads/2023/04/Characteristics-of-effective-and-fruitful-nonformal-theological-education.pdf.
———. "ICETE Manifesto on the Renewal of Evangelical Theological Education." Accessed 17 August 2022. http://www.icete-edu.org/manifesto.
——— "ICETE Manifesto II." 12 July 2022. https://icete.info/resources/manifesto/.
ICETE Academy. "Formal and Non-Formal Theological Education in Dialogue." https://icete.academy/course/view.php?id=172.
Increase Association. https://www.increaseassociation.org.
Jaison, Jessy. *Towards Vital Wholeness in Theological Education*. ICETE. Carlisle: Langham Global Library, 2017.
Jenkins, Philip. *The Next Christendom: The Coming of Global Christianity*. Oxford: Oxford University Press, 2007.
Jusu, John. "Reflections of TEE from Overseas Council in Africa." In *TEE for the 21st Century*, edited by David Burke, Richard Brown, and Qaiser Julius, 429–38. ICETE. Carlisle: Langham Global Library, 2021.
Kinsler, F. Ross. "Theological Education by Extension: Equipping God's People for Ministry." In *Ministry by the People: Theological Education by Extension*, edited by F. Ross Kinsler, 1–29. Maryknoll: Orbis, 1983.
Kraemer, Hendrick. *A Theology of the Laity*. Philadelphia: Westminster, 1975.
Kurlberg, Jonas, Nam Vo, and Sara Afshari. "Being Church in a Digital Age." Lausanne Occasional Paper for the Theology Working Group. Accessed 31 October 2022. https://lausanne.org/content/lop/lausanne-occasional-paper-being-church-in-a-digital-age?fbclid=IwAR2pwpH9lD1HE_3YSYJ_n7HGlyVRIiv9TbpfruzMbgXyOmJ0kE1ARKu70DM.
Lausanne Movement. "The Cape Town Commitment." 2010. https://lausanne.org/content/ctc/ctcommitment#capetown.

———. "Ministry Collaboration." Accessed 30 September 2022. https://lausanne.org/networks/issues/collaboration.

———. https://lausanne.org.

Law, Samuel. "Safeguarding the Church." Forum Comment, 17 November 2022. ICETE Academy Forum, ICETE Online Event, November 2021.

Lea, Jessica. "Max Lucado: The Church Needs the Holy Spirit, Not Another Program or Trend." Church Leaders. 12 September 2022. https://churchleaders.com/podcast/433631-max-lucado-church-needs-holy-spirit.html.

LeaderSource SGA (Strategic Global Assistance). https://www.leadersource.org.

———. https://www.leadersource.org/about/models.php.

Lloyd-Jones, Martyn. *Training Men for the Ministry Today*. London: London Theological Seminary, 1983.

Marsick, V. J., and K. Watkins. "Informal and Incidental Learning." In *The New Update on Adult Learning Theory: New Directions for Adult and Continuing Education*, edited by Sharan B. Merriam. San Francisco: Jossey-Bass, 2001.

McGavran, Donald A. "Foreword." In *Theological Education by Extension*, edited by Ralph D. Winter, xiii-xvi. Pasadena: William Carey Library, 1969.

Mulholland, Kenneth B. "A Modest Experiment Becomes a Model for Change." In *Christianity and Education: Shaping Christian Thinking in Context*, edited by David Emmanuel Singh and Bernard C. Farr, 33–41. Eugene: Wipf & Stock, 2011.

Ortiz, Michael A. "ICETE Begins Year of Conversation on Relations between Formal and Non-formal Education." WEA *Theological News* 51, no. 1 (Jan. 2022).

Ott, Bernhard. "Mission Oriented Theological Education: Moving beyond Traditional Models of Theological Education." In *Christianity and Education: Shaping Christian Thinking in Context*, edited by David Emmanuel Singh and Bernard C. Farr, 49–65. Eugene: Wipf & Stock, 2011.

Ott, Craig. "Globalizing Theology." In *Globalized Theology: Belief and Practice in an Era of World Christianity*, edited by Craig Ott and Harold A. Netland, 309–36. Grand Rapids: Baker Academic, 2007.

"Pastoral Trainers Declaration." Cape Town, South Africa. October 2010. https://rreach.org/wp-content/uploads/2017/05/Pastoral-Trainers-Declaration-Cape-Town-2010.pdf.

Perry, Abby. "Non-Traditional Seminary Students Are Changing the Church." CT Creative Studio, 7 January 2020. Accessed 1 October 2022. https://www.christianitytoday.com/partners/higher-education/non-traditional-seminary-students-are-changing-church.html.

Pickard, Stephen. *Theological Foundations for Collaborative Ministry*. London: Routledge, 2009.

Plueddemann, Jim E. "The Challenge of Excellence in Theological Education." In *Excellence and Renewal: Goals for Accreditation of Theological Institutions*, edited by Robert L. Youngblood, 1–14. Carlisle: Paternoster, 1989.

Pobee, John S. "Theology in the Context of Globalization." *Ministerial Formation* 79 (Oct. 1997): 18–26.

Poobalan, Dr. Ivor. "Plenary 4: The Landscape of Witness and Discipleship in the Digital Age." ATA General Assembly, Penang, 26–30 September 2022. Asia Theological Association. "Plenary Sessions" (2022). https://www.ataasia.com/2022ataga/plenary-sessions/.

Quintanilla, Milton. "World Evangelical Alliance Leader Warns That 'Bible Knowledge Is Fading Away.'" Christian Headlines. 4 December 2020. https://www.christianheadlines.com/contributors/milton-quintanilla/our-biggest-problem-is-that-bible-knowledge-is-fading-away-world-evangelical-alliance-leader-warns.html.

Re-Forma. "Outcomes." Accessed 24 August 2022. https://www.re-forma.global/outcomes.

Samuel, Vinay. "Globalization and Theological Education." In *Christianity and Education: Shaping Christian Thinking in Context*, edited by David Emmanuel Singh and Bernard C. Farr, 81–89. Eugene: Wipf & Stock, 2011.

Smith, Kevin. "Summary of the Cape Town Commitment." Lausanne Movement. 18 March 2011. Accessed 30 September 2022. https://lausanne.org/content/summary-of-the-cape-town-commitment.

Starkey, Mike. "Ivory Steeples?" *Third Way*, October 1989.

Tan, Jason Richard. "Matrices for Understanding Pastoral Leadership and Implications for the Global Landscape of Theological Education." *Insights Journal* 5, no. 1 (Nov. 2019): 33–47.

Theological Education Fund, *Ministry in Context: The Third Mandate Programme of the Theological Education Fund (1970-1977)* Bromley: TEF, 1972.

Thomas, Jaison. "Church Ministry Formation in Theological Education." PhD diss., Queen's University Belfast, 2008.

UNESCO Institute for Lifelong Learning. "The Global Observatory of Recognition, Validation and Accreditation of Non-formal and Informal Learning." Accessed 29 September 2022. https://uil.unesco.org/lifelong-learning/recognition-validation-accreditation.

United World Mission. https://uwm.org.

———. "Our Mission." Accessed 6 July 2022. https://uwm.org/about/our-mission/.

Van Engen, Charles E. "The Glocal Church: Locality and Catholicity in a Globalizing World." In *Globalized Theology: Belief and Practice in an Era of World Christianity*, edited by Craig Ott and Harold A. Netland, 157–79. Grand Rapids: Baker Academic, 2007.

Vanhoozer, Kevin J. "One Rule to Rule Them All? Theological Method in an Era of World Christianity." In *Globalized Theology: Belief and Practice in an Era of World Christianity*, edited by Craig Ott and Harold A. Netland, 85–126. Grand Rapids: Baker Academic, 2007.

van Wingerden, Hanna-Ruth, Tim Green, and Graham Aylett, eds. *TEE in Asia: Empowering Churches, Equipping Disciples*. ICETE. Carlisle: Langham Global Library, 2021.

Wayman, Benjamin D. "Imagining the Future of Theological Education." Conversations with Rowan Williams, Justo González, Emilie Townes, and Sam Wells. *The Christian Century*. 10 February 2021. https://www.christiancentury.org/article/features/imagining-future-theological-education.

Webber, Malcolm. *Healthy Evaluation Course Manual*. Elkhart: Strategic, 2010.

Werner, Dietrich. "Perspectives on the Future of Theological Education in Asia." In *Asian Handbook of Theological Education and Ecumenism*, edited by Hope Antone, Wati Longchar, et al., 657–66. Taiwan: PTCA, 2013.

White, James Emery. "The Ending of Seminaries as We've Known Them." Crosswalk. 6 June 2022. https://www.crosswalk.com/blogs/dr-james-emery-white/the-ending-of-seminaries-as-weve-known-them.html.

Winter, Ralph D. *Theological Education by Extension*. Pasadena: William Carey Library, 1969.

Wright, Chris. "Alertly Rooted! Energetically Engaged!" Keynote Address. ICETE Triennial, Nairobi, 2012.

Wright, N. T. *Broken Signposts: How Christianity Makes Sense of the World*. New York: HarperOne, 2020.

Yu, Carver. "Engaging the Ecclesial Dimension: Theological Education That Empowers the Church." In *The Pastor and Theological Education: Essays in Memory of Rev. Derek Tan*, edited by Siga Arles, Lily Lim, Tan-Chow Mayling, and Brian Wintle, 166–77. Singapore: Trinity Christian Center & ATA Bangalore, 2007.

Zurlo, Gina A. *Global Christianity: A Guide to the World's Largest Religion from Afghanistan to Zimbabwe*. Grand Rapids: Zondervan, 2022.

Global Hub for Evangelical Theological Education

Mission

ICETE advances quality and collaboration in global theological education to strengthen and accompany the church in its mission.

Objectives

As a global hub for evangelical theological education, ICETE is recognized for its reliable capacity to:

1. Develop, disseminate, mutually validate, harmonize, and inspire quality in theological education, aimed at fostering reciprocal trust among stakeholders, including the church;
2. Cultivate worldwide relationships, stimulated through gatherings, communications for reflection, interactive dialogue, collaboration, and practice in support of the church's mission; and
3. Train, consult, and provide resources for those involved in theological education, marked by relevance, accessibility, and collaborative effectiveness.

ICETE's mission emphasizes its dual focus on quality *and* collaboration through its constituency to strengthen and accompany the church in its mission. The quality aspect of our work addresses the church-academy gap by requiring theological institutions to build strategic partnerships with churches and ministry organizations. ICETE quality assurance seeks to be an agent for change in theological institutions, and consequently in the lives of the next generation of global leaders.

Through collaborative opportunities, our impact begins with theological educators and extends exponentially to training programs, students, church leaders, and the broader community for the sake of the church. Our work targets theological educators across all sectors who prepare thousands of learners serving in hundreds of ministries.

www.icete.info

Langham Literature and its imprints are a ministry of Langham Partnership.

Langham Partnership is a global fellowship working in pursuit of the vision God entrusted to its founder John Stott –

> *to facilitate the growth of the church in maturity and Christ-likeness through raising the standards of biblical preaching and teaching.*

Our vision is to see churches in the Majority World equipped for mission and growing to maturity in Christ through the ministry of pastors and leaders who believe, teach and live by the word of God.

Our mission is to strengthen the ministry of the word of God through:
- nurturing national movements for biblical preaching
- fostering the creation and distribution of evangelical literature
- enhancing evangelical theological education

especially in countries where churches are under-resourced.

Our ministry

Langham Preaching partners with national leaders to nurture indigenous biblical preaching movements for pastors and lay preachers all around the world. With the support of a team of trainers from many countries, a multi-level programme of seminars provides practical training, and is followed by a programme for training local facilitators. Local preachers' groups and national and regional networks ensure continuity and ongoing development, seeking to build vigorous movements committed to Bible exposition.

Langham Literature provides Majority World preachers, scholars and seminary libraries with evangelical books and electronic resources through publishing and distribution, grants and discounts. The programme also fosters the creation of indigenous evangelical books in many languages, through writer's grants, strengthening local evangelical publishing houses, and investment in major regional literature projects, such as one volume Bible commentaries like *The Africa Bible Commentary* and *The South Asia Bible Commentary*.

Langham Scholars provides financial support for evangelical doctoral students from the Majority World so that, when they return home, they may train pastors and other Christian leaders with sound, biblical and theological teaching. This programme equips those who equip others. Langham Scholars also works in partnership with Majority World seminaries in strengthening evangelical theological education. A growing number of Langham Scholars study in high quality doctoral programmes in the Majority World itself. As well as teaching the next generation of pastors, graduated Langham Scholars exercise significant influence through their writing and leadership.

To learn more about Langham Partnership and the work we do visit **langham.org**

www.ingramcontent.com/pod-product-compliance
Lightning Source LLC
Chambersburg PA
CBHW070806230426
43665CB00017B/2509